RAILWAYS
SINCE 1939

RAILWAYS SINCE 1939

by H. C. Casserley

David & Charles : Newton Abbot

385
1745

ISBN 0 7153 5487 6

Set in ten on eleven point Plantin
and printed in Great Britain
by W J Holman Limited Dawlish
for David & Charles (Publishers) Limited
South Devon House   Newton Abbot   Devon

Contents

Foreword

THIS BOOK is designed to have a wide range of appeal for those interested in railways in general, with particular accent on their changing status in the modern pattern of life. It also deals with more specialised subjects such as locomotive history, perhaps the major interest of any railway student, and the gradual change in the pattern of train services and railway facilities. The story is recounted of the effect on the railways of World War II, and the vital part they played in its prosecution, without which it is doubtful whether we could ever have survived.

This is not a detailed history of any of these aspects, each of which could easily be devoted to one or more volumes in itself. It is sometimes deliberately outspoken on contentious points, occasionally possibly controversial, but it does try to give a general overall picture interspersed with an occasional out-of-the-way anecdote, and also endeavours to present an easily readable narrative rather than a dry clinical record of events. The illustrations are carefully selected to give a general idea of the railways during the war years and the changes which have taken place since. Although more recent modern developments have not been neglected, these are comparatively fresh in memory and amply illustrated elsewhere. The emphasis therefore is rather on the general changing scene, and is mainly concerned with typical views over the last decade which is now rapidly becoming but a memory.

The War Years 1939-1945

THE FORERUNNER of this volume, 'Railways Between the Wars', to which this is intended as a sequel, finished on 3 September 1939 on the declaration of war by Great Britain and France against Germany.

The railways were well prepared to meet the emergency, as it had been apparent for some time, even before the Munich crisis of 1938, that such an event was at least more than likely, if not even inevitable. Churchill, with his far seeing wisdom, had of course appreciated this years before, but he was almost a lone voice crying in the wilderness. The country as a whole could not be made to realise the probability or even the possibility of a second conflict within a generation, preferring to bury its head in the sand after the proverbial manner of the ostrich.

By 1937, however, the Government had begun to realise the seriousness of the situation, and tentative plans were already being considered by the 'high-ups' in the railways for dealing with an emergency should it arise. The events of September 1938 brought things startlingly to the forefront, and the Ministry of Transport by an order dated 24 September 1938 appointed the Railway Executive Committee as an advisory body. It had powers to ensure that in a national crisis the operation of the railways and the London Transport Board should be used to the full in the interests of maintaining supplies and services essential to the life of the community.

The committee consisted of Sir Ralph Wedgwood of the LNER, who was elected chairman, Sir James Milne, GWR, as vice-chairman, together with Sir William Wood of the LMS, Mr Gilbert Szlumper from the SR and Mr Frank Pick of London Transport, with Mr G. Cole Deacon of the Railway Companies' Association, acting as secretary. After the signing of the Munich agreement on 4 October 1938, the committee met regularly to draw up emergency plans which could be put into operation at short notice, if and when another similar

situation should arise, which by the summer of 1939 was becoming more and more inevitable.

These plans included not only such obvious measures as withdrawal of luxury and unessential passenger train movements to allow for the conveyance of troops, air raid precautions, the question of restricted lighting owing to the black-out which would have to be enforced, plans for speedy repair of damage to railway property, and so on, but also a comprehensive programme of evacuating much of the civilian population from London and other large centres to country districts. This was put into operation between 1 and 4 September 1939 and involved the running of 3823 trains conveying over one and a quarter million women and children, of which over 600,000 were from Greater London, over 150,000 from Merseyside, about 120,000 from Glasgow and Clydebank, some 115,000 from Manchester, and correspondingly smaller numbers from other large centres of population. When the threatened air raids did not materialise during the first few months, many of the evacuees returned to their homes. But when the war hotted-up in earnest, further emergency schemes had to be devised, although on a smaller scale, 805 special trains being run in 1940, and 291 in 1941. When the flying bombs and rockets made their appearance 576 special trains were run in 1944 and 122 in 1945.

The Emergency Powers Defence Act of August 1939 empowered the Minister of Transport to take over the railways, and this was put into effect by the Emergency (Railway Control) Order of 1 September 1939. Under the order the Minister took control of the main line railways, London Transport, the Mersey Railway, Kings Lynn Docks & Railway Company, and, perhaps rather oddly, three of the late Colonel Stephens' famous light railways, the East Kent and the Kent & East Sussex, obviously by virtue of their geographical situation, and the Shropshire & Montgomeryshire, which was later put to war use by the construction of a large number of ammunition dumps along its route.

So far as the East Kent Railway was concerned, the reason for the Minister of Transport's interest in this otherwise relatively unimportant backwater (true it served a large colliery at Tilmanstone and one or two other smaller ones, but otherwise it was a little used country branch line) was the existence of the somewhat obscure port of Richborough. This had come into existence during World War I in 1916, when it was used as a goods train-ferry conveying wagons through to Calais and Dunkirk, a branch having been constructed by the East Kent Railway. During 1917 and 1918 the ferries had conveyed over one and a quarter million tons of heavy war supplies, including locomotives, guns and tanks, to the continent. On the cessation of hostilities, the port fell into disuse. It was again brought into commission in 1939, though on a smaller scale than before, and more as an alternative route in case of severe war damage at Dover or on the main line. Nevertheless it played its part in this important traffic until the fall of France, and is believed to have been to some extent used during the retreat from Dunkirk, after which it once more became redundant, this time for good.

The MoT's Emergency Act of 1 September 1939 also provided for the requisition of all privately owned wagons, of which there were some half a million. These were put into common usage, except for those designed for special traffics. On 11 September 1939 came drastic cuts in train services, including all restaurant car facilities and most sleeping cars, followed on 24 September by all special excursion trains and bookings. The Great Western was the first to publish a National Emergency Timetable, on 25 September 1939. The LMS and LNER had theirs ready, but undated and not issued to the public in advance. These revised services came into operation on 21 September.

Some relaxations were conceded during October, including the restoration of some restaurant cars and cheap day fares. The latter were again finally withdrawn on 5 October 1942, when the prosecution of the war was attaining its zenith, and non-essential passenger traffic was being discouraged as much as possible. Large posters appeared on the stations and in the press: 'Is your journey really necessary?' Later, in the final stages of the war, all remaining restaurant car services were to be withdrawn on 4 April 1944, under orders from the Minister of War Transport.

Apart from innumerable special trains which had

to be run for troop movements and the like, mention should be made of the special for naval personnel which ran daily between Euston and Thurso (referred to elsewhere). Another regular working, not so well known, was a special British Overseas Airways train which ran between Victoria and Poole between 1942 and 1945. It consisted of a bogie baggage van and four Pullman cars, and was usually worked by a T9 4–4–0. It was booked to run nonstop between Wimbledon and Poole, the longest non-stop run on the SR, and was presumably routed via Stewarts Lane Junction, Clapham Junction (Windsor side) and East Putney.

The threatened invasion scare by paratroops in 1940 resulted in the complete removal of all station nameboards, and signs of identification of locality—including of course road direction posts—which might have been of use to the enemy should this operation have been attempted. Black-out precautions had to be strictly observed. This entailed the provision of large hoods over the lights in the carriages, making reading very difficult except under the small central beam permitted—corner seats were no longer sought after! All blinds had to be drawn, a regulation very strictly enforced. Locomotives had to have their cabs screened to avoid the glare from the firebox, and colour light signals protected from visibility from above. The greatest problems of all occurred with outside movements, particularly shunting in marshalling yards at night, which became a most difficult and hazardous operation.

As it eventually turned out, the only part of the British Isles to be invaded by the enemy was the Channel Islands, occupied by the Germans on 1 July 1940. There had been two light railways on Jersey, one of standard gauge closed in 1929, and a narrow-gauge line which survived until 1937, after which it seemed extremely unlikely that any sort of railway would ever be seen there again. Nevertheless the Germans did in fact lay a metre-gauge line over part of the trackbed of the 3ft 6in Jersey Railway to serve an underground hospital and convey granite from quarries for coastal fortifications. It was worked by a number of tank engines of French origin. They also had a small 1ft 11½in gauge line at St Helier, worked by a diesel. Both of these were dismantled in 1946, and Jersey once more became an island without railways, this time doubtless for good.

The early days of the war involved the conveyance of thousands of troops to the ports, mainly the Expeditionary Force to France which largely went through Southampton, although others, and much of the equipment, stores, munitions in large quantities and tanks, passed through Dover, Harwich, Avonmouth and the South Wales ports. Reinforcements were also required for the Mediterranean and Middle East garrisons to bring them up to wartime strength; these were mainly dealt with through Clydeside and Merseyside. All this had been pre-arranged, and was carried out in a methodical and orderly fashion, the largest movements of the BEF taking place between 9 September and the early days of October, with a second large consignment from 7 January 1940 lasting about four weeks. The alarming deterioration in the position across the Channel in May 1940 lead to the cancellation on 11 May of all proposed additional holiday services, and the final collapse of France produced a severe and unexpected crisis which called for a reversal of this procedure so far as it was practicable. This had to be improvised at very short notice, and without any advance information as to where the returning ships from Dunkirk might arrive, or the numbers of troops involved. The magnificent way in which the railways rose to the occasion, the Southern in particular by reason of its geographical position, and handled this unprecedented situation, still stands as a marvel of organisation never before or since achieved in the annals of railway history.

The operation known as 'Dynamo' started on 27 May 1940, when no less than 186 complete trains comprising some two thousand coaches were assembled from all the main line railways and despatched to the various landing points so far as could be anticipated. The SR itself provided fifty-five of these trains, the LNER forty-seven, LMS forty-four, and GWR forty. Ships of all types and sizes had been hurriedly assembled at Dunkirk, the only port on the French side not already cut off by the German army, and the only possible means of escape for the BEF. Many of these were railway owned vessels, including all the cross Channel fleet of the Southern, those not already on war service being summarily commandeered by the Government on 29 May. There were also the Irish boats of the LMS and those from the LNER formerly serving the Netherlands and Scandinavia. The GWR quota not only consisted of the Channel Islands and Fishguard-Rosslare boats, but even the diminutive 'Mew' of the Dartmouth Ferry, which gallantly came to join in the rescue and survived to return to its former peaceful habitat. Bombing attacks were severe, and several ships were sunk, but nevertheless 319,000

troops were saved during this hectic nine days, and conveyed by 620 trains from the disembarkation ports to destinations all over the country by this remarkable 'Dynamo' operation.

All ordinary services had of course to be severely curtailed or even totally suspended over the lines leading to the ports. Dover and Folkestone had borne the brunt of this unprecedented traffic, and most of these trains travelled over the main line through Tonbridge, Redhill (where they had to reverse, with all its complications), Guildford and Woking (again an awkward point) for transfer to the LSWR, or more easily Reading, from where trains could be dispersed over the GWR system. Arrangements had to be made for feeding the weary troops. Headcorn, normally a small wayside station, was one of the points chosen for a halt for this purpose, the task being carried out by forty RASC troops assisted by about fifty local ladies, who worked continuously in long daily and nightly shifts throughout the nine days. Similar facilities were provided at Paddock Wood. There were also the problems of servicing the engines; much of this was done at Redhill, although sometimes it was found necessary to take water at Tonbridge. Although the trains themselves were provided by all four of the railways, no 'borrowed' locomotives worked east of Redhill, to which point a few GWR engines, nearly all Churchward 2–6–0s, worked through from Reading and beyond. Otherwise the traffic was handled entirely by SR engines.

When bombing raids began in June 1940 after the period of the 'phoney war' (so far as this country was concerned), it was natural that the railways, so vital to the country's communications, should be singled out for attacks. The effects of these ranged from comparatively minor results, such as failure of telephone communications or other matters which could be rectified with comparative ease, to damage to track, bridges, stations or signal boxes, which in varying degrees could disrupt traffic for periods of a few hours to several days, according to its nature and extent. Lord Stamp, chairman of the LMS, was killed in an air raid at his home at Shortlands on 16 April 1941, an early and regrettable personal casualty from a railway standpoint. He had done much to further the interests of the LMS company since his initial appointment as President and the Executive Manager in 1926, and he was widely liked and respected by all grades. His death was a great blow both to the railway and to the country at large.

Damage to rolling stock was naturally on a large

9

scale, particularly to carriages and wagons, but a robust thing like a locomotive takes a good deal of disintegrating, and perhaps not surprisingly there were only eight cases of engines being damaged completely beyond repair. These included a former LSWR Drummond 4–6–0 No 458, which received a direct hit in Nine Elms shed in October 1940. Other cases were at York on 29 April 1942 (Gresley A4 Pacific No 4469 *Sir Ralph Wedgwood*), at Norwich in June 1942 (M & GNJ 4–4–0 No 047), at Devonport in June 1941 (GWR 4–6–0 No 4911 *Bowden Hall*) and Caledonian 4–4–0 No 14356 at Ladyburn in the same year. A Brighton 0–4–4T No 2365 was attacked by a German plane and badly damaged, but was nevertheless repaired. In the last stages of the war came the flying bombs, and finally the V2 rockets, Hitler's last throw, which played such havoc, mostly in areas in and around London at which they were directed. One of these fiendish contraptions managed to achieve a direct hit in 1944 at Stratford on a Great Eastern J17 class 0–6–0 No 8200, former GER 1200. Censorship was necessarily very tight at the time about this new menace, but in railway circles the rumour had somehow got round that this particular engine had been destroyed at Stratford 'owing to collision with a V2'. To the railway hierarchy, this would of course be interpreted as a fairly normal accident involving a Gresley 'Green Arrow' 2–6–2, and it was not until much later that the true facts were established!

Destruction to rolling stock was much more severe, no less than 637 passenger coaches and 3,321 wagons and vans of various kinds having to be written off as damaged beyond repair. Between 19 June 1940 and 27 March 1945 occurred a total of 9,239 'incidents' (a masterly description as regards some of the major upheavals), but the comparative importance of many of these can best be summarised as follows:

'Incidents' having little or no effect	3,618

This reduced the somewhat large total by over one third, leaving the important effects of air raid damage at a much lower figure.

1. 'Incidents' causing failure of telephone communication	528
2. Traffic facilities affected for up to six hours	1,132
3. Traffic facilities affected for six to twenty-four hours	1,595
4. Traffic facilities affected twenty-four hours to a week	662
5. Traffic facilities affected a week or over	247
6. Traffic facilities affected by presence of delayed action or unexploded bombs	1,457

By far the greater proportion of 'incidents' occurred during 1940 and 1941, after which they fell greatly, but with another peak in 1944 on the advent of the flying bombs and rockets. Obvious objectives from the enemy's point of view were the large railway centres such as Stratford in London. While Crewe, Derby, Darlington, Swindon and Eastleigh, such essential railway towns, did indeed receive due attention, it was nothing like on the scale which might have been expected. The main massive attacks was concentrated on the ports, Hull, Liverpool, Glasgow, Southampton and so on, not forgetting Coventry, neither a port nor a railway town. Marshalling yards such as Feltham and March received a full share of attention, probably because they were more easily identifiable from the air. Among the many major bomb damage 'incidents' may be noted as typical of the most serious (but there were of course many others):

26 September 1940 and again on 1 October 1940	Marylebone–St John's Wood tunnel. Initial repairs enabled trains again to work into Marylebone on 26 November 1940, but final repairs were not completed until August 1941.
20 December 1940 and again on 3 May 1941	Exchange Station, Liverpool.
19 April 1941	Blackfriars Bridge, damaged by parachute mine. Main track reopened in May and June, but permanent reconstruction not completed until 1942.
10 May 1941	St Pancras badly damaged, but traffic restored partly by 17 May and completed by 7 June.
29 April 1942	York, damaging Gresley Pacific No 4469 and NER B16 Class 4–6–0 No 925 beyond repair.
25 May 1943	Viaduct at Brighton on Lewes lines. Three piers demolished; temporary reconstruction completed by 29 June, and finished within four months.
13 June 1944	First damage by flying bomb (V1) at Coburn Road (GER); repairs completed by 17 June.

There were to be many other such 'incidents', most-ly in the London area, by these contraptions, and their far more deadly successor, the V2, one of which has already been referred to.

An important consideration which had to be con-stantly kept to the forefront was the vital necessity of maintaining adequate rail communications be-tween the south of England, particularly the Chan-nel ports, and the north. Especially vulnerable were the crossing points of the Thames in the London area, in respect of which there were four practicable routes only—the Metropolitan widened lines and over Blackfriars Bridge, the East London Railway, the West London Extension, and the SR at Kew Bridge, easily accessible from the North Western and Midland main lines over the North and South Western Junction Railway. Putney Bridge would have been quite impracticable for freight traffic as it could only be reached over the lines of the Met-ropolitan District and Metropolitan underground lines. Of these four, only the East London was in tunnel, the others being very much exposed to air attack. Several new loops and connections between adjacent lines were therefore put in at suitable points, not only in the London area itself, but away from the metropolis, so that in the event of any of the vital links being out of action, traffic could easily be diverted over one of the others. Among the most important of these were at Harringay and Gospel Oak, giving easy interchange between the LNER and LMS via the Tottenham & Hampstead Joint line. Out in the country a new loop at Calvert provided connection between the old Great Central main line and the LNWR from Bletchley to Oxford, where an-other new junction joined up with the Great West-ern. At the eastern end of this important cross-country link between Oxford and Cambridge a new north curve was put in at Sandy to provide for direct running between the LNWR and the Great Northern main line. Another important new loop at Canterbury gave connection between the former SER and LCDR lines, previously physically isolated. All of these connections proved invaluable at the height of the bombing raids when many lines were put temporarily out of action.

Travelling conditions over long distances became progressively more unpleasant as the war progress-ed, the East Coast main line between London and Edinburgh being particularly notorious. Notwith-standing huge trains of twenty or more coaches, overcrowding to an intolerable degree became com-monplace. One of the most miserable journeys I have ever made was in 1944 between King's Cross and Newcastle; with numerous stops and poor run-ning it took nearly nine hours and seemed intermin-able. The corridors were so tightly wedged that even access to the lavatories seemed out of the question, and when dire necessity made one literally force one's way along it would only be to find the place already jammed with several other passengers, one of whom would be taking advantage of having found some sort of seating accommodation, even if not us-ing it for its intended purpose! Privacy was there-fore out of the question. This must have happened on many occasions, and could produce difficulties where both sexes were involved, although most passengers had reached the point of no longer car-ing about such refined niceties of civilisation. I re-collect that on this occasion it was perhaps fortunate that the female contingent comprised a couple of WAAFs on leave, who were broad minded enough to be amused rather than embarrassed, but one can only speculate what would have happened if starchy Victorian Aunty Prudence had been among those present! There was of course no restaurant car, and if there had been it would have been useless because of its inaccessibility. I never got back to my com-partment during the journey and was lucky to find my bag still on the rack when the train partially cleared at Newcastle. Fortunately it was not yet closing time, and I think the couple of pints which I downed in about five minutes were among those which I have ever most enjoyed.

So the prosecution of the war proceeded, with the railways playing their vital part; without them it is difficult to see how the country could ever have survived. For one thing, we were almost entirely dependent on but assured of abundant coal supplies as a natural gift. Compare this with our present petrol and oil position, when our very existence both on rail and road is so much dependent on provision of our abundant needs from overseas sources. As the Anglo-American air striking force grew in in-tensity so the demands on the railways grew in transporting the necessary petrol and bombs to the airfields. A raid by a thousand American heavy bombers over Germany would, for instance, neces-sitate the provision of about 2,600,000 gallons of petrol, carried in 650 tank cars, with 2,900 tons of bombs in 362 wagons, making some twenty-eight trains in all. During 1944 alone some 927,000 tons of bombs were unloaded on the enemy by RAF Bomber Command and nearly 402,000 tons by the USA Eighth Air Force based in Britain—a simple

11

arithmetical calculation will indicate the size of the required effort.

The last tremendous task before victory was finally achieved at the time of the invasion of France. General (as he then was) Montgomery gave a talk under conditions of the greatest secrecy to selected railwaymen of all grades at Euston on 22 February 1944 outlining the plans for the operation known as 'Overlord', or D-Day as it eventually became. He concluded with the words, 'I am confident that I can rely on you giving your utmost co-operation in providing the necessary transport for the forces, so that when the final blow is struck it will be of the utmost possible intensity and lead to complete victory'.

There followed intensive preparation by the railways in co-operation with the War Office, for the movement of thousands of our American allies from the British ports at which they were arriving by convoy, together with transportation and movement of the immense amount of stores and heavy equipment required for the operation. This involved another 800 special trains, comprising 30,000 wagons, including 7,000 conveying tanks, these in themselves being awkward to fit in with the general movement as they were out of gauge loads and required special working arrangements. Nevertheless, every one reached its intended destination on time, and moreover with very little disruption to ordinary traffic, once more a remarkable feat of organisation. In the three weeks prior to actual D-Day, 6 June 1944, 9,679 special trains were run, of which 3,636 were in one single week at the height of the operation.

For the enormous upsurge in traffic during the war years, a great increase in the number of locomotives and wagon stock was of course essential, notwithstanding the pruning of ordinary services which enabled the provision of any additional purely passenger rolling stock to be kept to a minimum. For a start, it was necessary, as in World War I, to dispatch a large quantity of rolling stock to France along with the British Expeditionary Force, all of which had to be left behind in the retreat from Dunkirk. This principally comprised seventy-nine GWR Dean 0–6–0s out of a total of 108 of the class which had been taken over by the War Department in September 1939. The remainder were put to work at the various WD depots set up all over the country. One of these establishments was a large Ordnance Depot in the Oxfordshire countryside five miles from Bicester, where the author was a somewhat unwilling guest of His Majesty's Forces

from 1942-1944. Over this five-mile long railway, almost our only communication with the outside world, worked various War Department engines, including two of the Dean 0–6–0s among other oddments, a LNWR 2–4–2T 6725 and a LSWR Adams 0–4–2 No 625. The camp train consisted of a delightful selection of coaching stock, among which was a Highland and a Glasgow & South Western bogie third, and a Midland clerestory, a collection which would cause raptures among the preservationists of today but was thought very little of at that time. This train normally ran only into a siding at Bicester yard but there was a Saturdays only recreational train through to Oxford LMS, worked throughout by WD engines and men unpiloted.

Some of the GWR 0–6–0s had already served in a similar capacity in France during World War I, and were now 'called up' for a second time. Those lost in France on this occasion were naturally used by the German occupation forces. A few survived to be returned here after the termination of hostilities, but were found to be unfit for further service and were broken up. To replace the loss of all these engines, the LMS loaned to the GWR forty of their Johnson class 2 0–6–0s and the LNER forty of their North Eastern somewhat similar J21 type engines.

History repeated itself on a small scale in World War II. During both wars a number of engines which had been withdrawn from service during the preceding months and laid aside in case of emergency were reinstated to do further valuable service. These included some classes which would have become extinct but were given a further lease of life. Again, some railways found themselves so acutely short of engine power that they had to borrow from some of those less affected. Once more the Highland line was one of these because of its great increase in traffic owing to the presence of the Navy at Scapa Flow. This involved among other things the running of a through train daily between Euston and Thurso for the benefit of the Navy personnel. The HR section had to borrow anything it could get hold of, among which may be mentioned some G & SWR 2–6–0s that were shedded at Tain. Also, once more, engines from the south were to be seen in the north of Scotland. During World War I these had consisted of such unlikely things as three LSWR 4–4–2Ts which appeared on the Kyle of Lochalsh line, and Brighton 'Terriers' at Invergordon. This time some Brighton 0–4–2Ts were sent to Scotland, one of which reached the Highland and was used on the Wick & Lybster branch. It is a great pity that, so far as is known, no photograph was secured, or at any rate has survived, of this interesting event of a Southern engine being at work on Britain's most remote line from London. (The branch itself was entirely closed in April 1944, just prior to the end of the war).

Photography was a difficult and hazardous proceeding in those days, and the north of Scotland was in any case a prohibited area to the ordinary traveller during the war. The actual position regarding photography was none too clear, the regulations on the subject prohibiting taking photographs of 'anything of a warlike nature'. It seemed that on the face of it that one would be in order in taking an innocent photograph of a locomotive and train (but beware of taking, say, an ammunition train with a tank or guns mounted on a wagon), but in practice one found that the police and plain clothes detectives did not usually take so liberal a view. After narrowly escaping arrest on two occasions I had more or less to give up the attempt unless being quite sure I was unobserved, but I had to miss some tantalisingly unique subjects in consequence.

To come back to the locomotive position in general, 1941 saw the necessity of finding further engines for service overseas. This time the LNER provided 92 of its Robinson 2–8–0s, which had been adopted as a standard design by the War Department during World War I, when several hundred had been built to the requirements of what was at that time known as the Railway Operating Division. As in the case of the GWR 0–6–0s some of these 2–8–0s were actually the same engines which had seen war service in the previous conflict. These LNER engines went to the Middle East, and never came back. Meanwhile the Ministry of Transport had decreed that in the interests of economy and standardisation all new freight engines constructed by the four groups should be of the LMS Stanier 8F design, which had already amply proved its worth on the parent company. Thus it came about that these engines were built in large numbers, not only at Crewe and Horwich, but also at Swindon, Darlington, Doncaster, Eastleigh, Brighton and Ashford, in addition to which further orders were placed 'outside' with the North British Locomotive Company. A particularly interesting example of the sort of thing that could now happen was the construction at Brighton in 1944 of a batch of the LMS type 2–8–0s for the LNER! Initially Nos 7651-7675, later renumbered 3100-3124, then 3500-3524, they were

transferred (or sold?) to the LMS in 1947, on which line they became Nos 8705-8729. All this was of course before nationalisation. Other engines of this design were sent to the Middle East on war service but a few eventually returned to this country. It might be mentioned at this point that the railway companies' own workshops were not only concerned with the repair and building of locomotives, but some sections of the works were also turned over to the construction of tanks and aeroplane parts.

In 1943 a new design of 2–8–0 known as the 'Austerity' was introduced mainly for war service, and no less than 935 were built by the North British Locomotive Company and the Vulcan Foundry. This was almost the largest number of engines ever built in this country to a single design, just short of the total of 943 of Ramsbottom's DX 0–6–0s which had been built for the LNWR and L&YR three quarters of a century earlier between 1858 and 1874. Although owned by the War Department, many of the new engines were loaned to the railways until they were required for war service by the authorities. A larger version with the 2–10–0 wheel arrangement also appeared in the same year, 150 being built by the North British Locomotive Company between 1943 and 1945. Both of these designs should be accredited to Mr R. A. Riddles, associated at that time with the Ministry of Supply, and who was destined to become BR's last steam Chief Mechanical Engineer.

Concurrently with the above, we began to receive supplies of 2–8–0s from the USA under the Lease Lend plan, when that country became actively engaged in the war after Pearl Harbour. These were of typical American design, many features, such as bar frames, being almost unknown in this country apart from the importation of some 2–6–0s by the MR, GNR, and GCR at the turn of the century, which had short lives. A lot of these 2–8–0s again put in a great deal of service over the main lines, while others were seen just briefly passing through on their way from Liverpool to the continent or Middle East. At one time there was a large dump of them in South Wales, none of which was ever steamed during their sojourn in this country. These engines were built by the Baldwin Locomotive Company, American Locomotive Company and Lima Locomotive Company.

For general short distance and shunting duties at WD depots, a useful type of 0–6–0ST was introduced by the Ministry of Supply in 1943, of which several hundred were turned out by outside builders, Hunslet, Stephenson & Hawthorn, Hudswell Clark, Bagnall, and the Vulcan Foundry. After the end of the war they were widely dispersed. The LNER took 75 of them, but they were also eagerly sought after by collieries and other industrial concerns and, where not supplanted by diesels, some may still be seen at work to-day. The corresponding USA version of the shunting—or, in the language of that country, 'switching'—engine was an 0–6–0T of distinctive American appearance with outside cylinders. Many came to this country although few actually worked here. These engines were built by the Vulcan Locomotive Works (USA), Davenport Locomotive Works, and H. K. Porter & Co. After the war the Southern acquired fourteen of them to replace their aged 0–4–0Ts for shunting in Southampton Docks, and happily some of these have been acquired by preservation societies, one of them being on the Keighley & Worth Valley Railway.

Apart from these WD types built specially for wartime purposes, new construction and even new designs were very naturally at a minimum during the war years. Sir Nigel Gresley introduced a new lightweight three cylinder 2–6–2 intended for general purpose duties, but only two were built, and Edward Thompson, who succeeded him, preferred a simpler and more robust design of two cylinder 4–6–0 for a mixed traffic engine, the well known B1 class, the first of which appeared in 1942.

On the Southern, Mr O. V. Bulleid, who had succeeded Mr Maunsell in 1937 as Chief Mechanical Engineer, startled the locomotive world by two entirely new and distinctly unconventional designs. In 1941, at the height of the war, he somehow managed to produce what was no less than a new design of top link express passenger engines, the 'Merchant Navy' pacific. One wonders how he got this past the board of directors, let alone the Ministry of Transport. Was it by maintaining that it was somehow essential to the war effort? However favourably prejudiced, one cannot in all honesty accept, in

retrospect, that this was the case, but at least it put steam on the Southern again for another decade.

This railway had built no express passenger engines since the last batch of 'Schools' in 1935, and it was beginning to appear that it might be seriously considering the abandonment of steam for main line work, with thoughts presumably turned in the direction of electrification, or even diesels, already beginning to be established as a practical proposition. This might well have happened but for the forceful personality of Mr Bulleid, who described himself unequivocally as an out and out 'steam dog', stemming no doubt from his association with Sir Nigel Gresley, under whom he had worked for many years at Doncaster before coming to the Southern. Until his arrival on the scene it was certainly never envisaged that this railway was likely to embark on a pacific design, and that there would ultimately be no less than 140 engines of this type, far eclipsing the more modest total of fifty-one on the LMS. The various LNER designs eventually exceeded 200 by 1949, the last examples coming out after nationalisation, while the Great Western had of course never repeated the example of its solitary pacific Great Bear of 1908.

Shortly after the appearance of the first Merchant Navy, Mr Bulleid again captured the headlines in the railway press, then under somewhat severe censorship restrictions, by the appearance from Brighton in 1942 of the first Q1 0–6–0s, which quickly earned for themselves the dubious distinction of being the ugliest engines ever seen in this country. This was perhaps a slight exaggeration, but certainly not far from the truth, although they were extremely efficient and of great use in helping to cope with the difficult wartime conditions. On other railways new construction was confined to well tried and established mixed traffic types, such as the LMS 'Black Fives' and the Great Western 'Halls' (turned out without names—these were added after the termination of the war).

14

The Immediate Post-War Years 1945-1947

8 MAY 1945—VE day (Victory in Europe). The unconditional surrender of Germany after nearly six years of unremitting toil—blood, sweat and tears—when more than once our fate hung in a very fine balance, and when without the leadership and inspiration of Winston Churchill things might very well have gone the other way.

15 August 1945—VJ Day (Victory in Japan), and for a time at least the world was to be free from the horrors of war.

The railways had done a magnificent job with superb organisation, but with the effect that they were naturally in an extremely run down condition. When they came under scrutiny by the new Labour government, all the thanks they got from at least one quarter was the waspish comment that they were a 'pretty poor bag of assets'. It was conveniently forgotten that the railways had made large profits for the government during the war. Gratitude has indeed never been a notable feature of the average human make-up, but never was this more exemplified than the nation's decision—still never satisfactorily explained, although many theories have been put forward—that Churchill should no longer lead the country now that the crisis was over. This quite overlooked the fact that, had we been defeated, such of us as would have survived at all would at least be living a life of subjection, or a fate 'worse than death'.

However, there it was, and it was to have a far reaching effect on the history of railways in this country. The socialist government, once in power, lost little time in proceeding to further plans to satisfy one of its long standing ambitions, national ownership of the major industries. Even so, there is little doubt that the economic position would eventually have necessitated some form of overall amalgamation, whether under state control or otherwise. Herbert Morrison announced in the House of Commons on 19 November 1945 the Government's intentions under which the railways, coal and steel, were to be taken as first priority. The mining industry was the first to be dealt with, the hitherto privately owned collieries all coming under state ownership by the formation of the National Coal Board, which came into operation on 1 January 1947.

Meanwhile plans for the unification of the entire British railway system, with a few minor exceptions, together with the canal and inland navigation undertakings, shipping, harbours and port facilities, into one state owned concern to be known as the British Transport Commission, had been proceeding apace. This culminated in the Transport Act 1947, 10 and 11 GEO 6, Chapter 49, the Bill being passed on 6 August 1947. It was of mammoth proportions, the printed Act comprising 170 pages and the main part being divided into 128 sections, many with numerous sub-headings, together with fifteen schedules dealing with such matters as the terms of transfer of railway and canal securities to be replaced by British Transport stock, compensation for the acquisition of privately owned wagons, and so on. Further consideration of the new set-up and the many changes which were inevitable will be described in the next chapter dealing with the period 1948-1955, but meanwhile we can take a look at the various happenings during the intervening period after the cessation of hostilities.

All the railways endeavoured to restore something like pre-war conditions as quickly as possible. For instance, restaurant car facilities were restored on the LMS, LNER and Southern on 1 October 1945, followed by the GWR on 31 December, and in May of the following year some attempt was made to reintroduce summer services, comprising many extra trains and accelerated timings. The travelling postal sorting offices, with lineside apparatus for the exchange of mail bags at high speed, which had been discontinued since September 1939, were restored on 1 October 1945 between Euston-Aberdeen and Paddington-Penzance, followed on 6 May 1946 by the Bristol-Newcastle, Newcastle-Kings Cross, Kings Cross-York-Edinburgh and other services.

Nevertheless, the years of 'make do and mend' could not be put right overnight, and it took time to overcome the accumulated results of lack of maintenance. There could be no question for the moment of attempting to go back to the immediate pre-war standards of punctuality and reliability, let alone any really high speed services. Of all the main lines out of London, I think the old LNWR was perhaps the most unfortunate. Having lived since 1939 (with a short gap in the early war years) in a house overlooking the line at Berkhamsted, I have been able to enjoy a grandstand view of all that has been going on from the earlier days, when it was by far the most fascinating of all main lines, through the gradual introduction of diesel traction down to the present time, which with its ultra efficient electric operation is the least interesting to the observer.

It is interesting now to look back on the immediate post-war period as an indication of the general conditions of travel at that time. Most railways had to contend with war engines in poor shape owing to lack of maintenance. The very poor quality of coal available was possibly the most important factor of all, while in the case of the old LNWR one must regret to say there was a not too efficient standard of operation exercised by the control organisation. It was interesting to watch the morning procession of overnight trains from the north and observe the conditions operating. On a good day the Glasgow sleeper, due in at 6.45 am would pass on time, with, say, 6245 *City of London* going well, followed with any luck by the Perth and others and, finally, the Inverness, due 8.30, all appearing more or less to schedule. But too often it was a different story. One failure on a lonely stretch, say at Grayrigg, could cause havoc, not only to the offending train, but also to those following which were stacking up behind, while a second failure (by no means an unknown event with the same train, the replacement engine possibly being nothing more than an ailing class 5 with almost unburnable coal) could be disastrous. When I was daily commuting up to London, I would make a point of visiting the rather grandiose arrival indicator which appeared somewhere about 1950, situated in what was rather like a small cinema hall in which one could sit and watch the progress of things (this is now of course all swept away). On some of the more unfortunate days the panels would read more like the score board of a test match— 104 late at Carlisle, Crewe 126 late, latest score 171 not out (or should one say not in yet!) at Nuneaton, and so on. In a way it was great entertainment for the observer, but not so for the unfortunate passengers, perhaps two or three hours late and marooned with no opportunity of obtaining any sustenance. One of these occasions which stands out in my mind was the up Glasgow sleeper, headed by a very tired looking LNWR G2 0–8–0, obviously all that had been available at some point en route, piloted by a London based 2–6–4T, probably attached at Bletchley. With a little imagination this might have been coupled 'inside' next to the train, where it could have provided much wanted steam heating, as it was midwinter, but apparently no one thought of this.

In defence of my perhaps severe strictures, I would say that the outer suburban service to Tring, Bletchley and Northampton was at that period commendably good and comfortable in the busy rush hour period (it was very thin at other times). It was one of the best in the greater London area, even if time keeping was liable to be a bit erratic. This was due to the fact that it was to some extent worked by wheezing Prince of Wales class 4–6–0s which had only been reprieved from scrap at the beginning of the war, and which had to manage with as little attention as possible. Their eventual withdrawal and replacement by class 5 4–6–0s effected a great improvement, although regretted on purely sentimental grounds.

The years 1945 and onwards saw a resumption in locomotive construction by all four groups on something approaching normal conditions, and several new designs appeared. On the LNER, Mr Thompson, who had succeeded Sir Nigel Gresley on the latter's death in 1941, had very different ideas from his predecessor. Following his B1 type 4–6–0s which had appeared during the war, he introduced in 1945 a new design of suburban 2–6–4T No 9000, of which one hundred examples were eventually built, most of them after nationalisation. They would have been ideal for the Great Eastern inner suburban services with short inter-station distances and frequent stops, but they came too late, as electrification was already under way, the first section from Liverpool Street to Shenfield being brought into operation on 26 September 1949. Most of their time was consequently spent on outer services such as Southend, Hitchin, Aylesbury and around Hull and Darlington, for which duties their 5ft 2in driving wheels were found to be on the small side for fast running. Thompson also introduced a new class of pacific, as well as embarking on a rebuilding programme of some of Gresley's designs, and certain of Robinson's also inherited from the Great Central. This came to an end in 1946, when he was succeeded by Mr A. H. Peppercorn, the LNE's last CME, a completely different kind of personality. From all accounts Mr Thompson had not been easy to get on with or to work under,* whereas Mr Peppercorn, a genial and kindly man, quickly gained the respect and affection of his staff and all who came into contact with him. I still have in my possession a charming letter, signed by him personally, readily agreeing to what was a simple formal application to visit Gorton works in 1948. His chief work in these last years was to increase the LNER's splendid fleet of pacifics by a further forty–nine based primarily on a Thompson rebuild of the original Gresley engine *Great Northern* of 1922. This engine ran for a year or two after 1945 in its re built form in an experimental livery which was not proceeded with—a dark royal blue very like the old Great Eastern.

On the LMS, Mr H. A. Ivatt became its last CME in 1945, and he introduced three new designs just before nationalisation; a light-weight 2–6–0, with a corresponding 2–6–2T version, and a heavier general purpose mixed traffic 2–6–0, all of which were not only built in considerable numbers, but adapted with very slight modifications by British Railways as three of their twelve standard designs. On the Great Western, Mr Hawksworth produced a new class of 4–6–0 with all the typical GWR characteristics of the previous forty years, together with the ultimate development of the inside cylinder 0–6–0 saddle/pannier tanks which had been such an essential feature of all parts of the Great Western scene ever since the 1870s. Since the first examples had appeared in 1860, over 2,000 had been built to many varying designs. Two hundred and ten of this final version appeared between 1947 and 1956 (the ultimate ones being the last engines to be built to a pre-nationalisation design), but these were destined to have a very short life owing to the rapid advance of dieselisation for yard shunting and short distance passenger and freight service.

On the SR, Mr Bulleid continued with his *Merchant Navies* and a slightly lighter version with wider route availability. An epoch making event however was the appearance at the close of 1947 of LMS No 10000, Britain's first diesel-electric main-line locomotive. Its significance was barely appreciated at the time, it being regarded as an interesting experiment with considerable possibilities within a limited range. The revolutionary changes in the picture of the British rail system which were to follow during the ensuing decade were certainly at that time hard-

ly to be imagined.

In 1946 there was a very severe coal shortage, so serious that all four railways embarked under Government direction on an extensive plan for conversion to oil burning, this being on a far more ambitious scale than anything previously attempted. Some twelve hundred engines were to have been adapted, and it was nobody's fault, indeed it could hardly have been foreseen at the time, that before the scheme got well underway circumstances entirely changed. Before many months had passed it was not coal that was in short supply so much as dollars, necessary to import oil from America, and it is therefore not surprising that the scheme was almost stillborn.

The Great Western and the Southern were the first to get going, on the latter line one of the classes selected being the evergreen fifty-year-old T9 4–4–0s, still going strong. This term could now only be used in the figurative sense, as the engines were then painted in war time black. This had been an economy measure on all four groups, universally applied to all classes, but soon after the end of the war the GWR announced a return to green, as did the SR with its very attractive shade of malachite. The LNER even went a little further in proposing to paint all classes in the well known apple green as a reaction against the drabness of the war time years, starting with the repainting of the 0–6–0T station pilots at York, Newcastle and Edinburgh. This was a very sensible idea as these engines were very much in the public eye, and were kept in spick and span condition. As far as widespread application was concerned however, it was really a wasted effort. The absence of cleaning, a luxury which had to be virtually abandoned during the war years, was unfortunately destined to persist, except in the case of top link passenger engines, not only through to nationalisation, but to a large extent right down to the end of steam. This resulted in the deplorable conditions which became progressively commonplace in more recent years. The majority of less important engines hardly ever saw the application of a cleaning rag between one repaint and another. These conditions varied between different areas, and it is pleasing to be able to record that in 1947 the smartest turn out of engines was to be found on the old Great North of Scotland shed at Kittybrewster, Aberdeen, which somehow managed to maintain every engine to pre-war sparkling standards of cleanliness. This state of affairs was, however, practically unique at the time.

*Mr Thompson's personality and his railway career have been amply detailed in a recent book by Peter Grafton.

B

1948 Onwards, Years of Nationalisation

ON 1 JANUARY 1948, whether we liked it or not, the day of the privately owned railway company was over, never to return. The old titles with which we had become familiar during the past twenty-five years, the LMS, LNER, GWR and SR, were swallowed up in what was then known as the Railway Executive. Eventually they would disappear altogether, although they could hardly be wiped out physically overnight. This must inevitably be a gradual process extending over years, but ultimately they would remain only in memory. They could, however, officially (although not legally) cease to exist forthwith, and so they did. After tidying their accounts and proving that all their assets had been transferred to the BTC, the SR was not legally wound up until 10 June 1949 and the others on 23 December 1949. On the financial side, at the beginning of 1947, the last year of independent operation, the market value of the Ordinary Stock of the respective companies stood as follows:

		Amount of stock (millions)
LMSR	30½	£95
LNER (Preferred)	6⅞	42
„ (Deferred)	3⅜	36
GWR	58	43
SR (Preferred)	6½	28
„ (Deferred)	24	31

The net revenues for the year 1946 for the four railways were:

LMS	£15,923,680
LNER	£11,078,471
GWR	£7,467,390
SR	£7,184,536

Shareholders at the Great Western's last company meeting insisted on giving its directors compensation, for which they did not ask. On the other hand, the LNER directors requested such compensation, which that company's shareholders refused.

It was no longer the London Midland & Scottish Railway, but the London Midland Region. This, for a start, comprised most lines of the former LMS company in England and Wales, but those in Scotland, together with the LNER system north of the border, became a separate entity for administrative purposes, the Scottish Region. In England itself, the old LNER was divided into two: the Eastern Region, roughly from south of Leeds and Doncaster, including East Anglia, and the North Eastern Region which was very largely what had been the old North Eastern Railway of pregrouping days. The Western Region still corresponded to the map of the Great Western Railway, as did the Southern Region with what had been the Southern Railway ever since 1923. All of these had sundry small additions of what had until 1947 still been independent railways, such as the Mersey, and sundry joint lines like the Cheshire Lines and others, now all incorporated into the London Midland Region. Similarly many light railways finally lost their independence, for example the East Kent and the Kent & East Sussex became merged into the Southern Region. During 1948/9 the former railway owned canals were transferred to the Docks & Inland Waterways Executive, which had at first been included in the Railway Executive.

The London Passenger Transport Board was now the London Transport Executive, continuing as a separate organisation for operation and maintenance. On 23 January 1950 it took over certain joint lines and sections of line in the London area formerly owned by the main line railways, such as the M & GC Joint line from Harrow to Verney Junction, the East London, LNER lines to High Barnet etc (already worked by Northern line trains of LT), the eastern section of the Central line to Epping, and other similar railways in the London area.

This was the first of sundry adjustments to be made in the areas covered by the separate regions, and was followed by a number of others which took effect from 2 April 1950. Some of these were entirely logical, such as the self-contained former London Tilbury & Southend Railway which had, owing to its absorption by the enterprising Midland Railway in 1912, found itself outside the sphere of its natural area (as indeed it had done ever since the grouping in 1923). It was at last transferred to the Eastern Region, where it obviously belonged.

Again, the lines in Devon and Cornwall, previously intermingled between the Great Western and

Southern Railways, represented a case for obvious transfer to one or other of the new regions. After some intershuffling between the two they ultimately became all Western. Other adjustments in the southern counties, such as the GWR Weymouth line to the Southern Region, were of a more dubious nature. The Somerset & Dorset Joint line even became involved with three regions. Such divisions involved unnecessary complication in the running of through trains by separate operating administrations. This consideration of course applied also to through trains between Waterloo and Plymouth, Ilfracombe, etc, and even more to the Anglo-Scottish services, which had been so divided right from the start of nationalisation. But with such natural 'frontiers' as Exeter, Carlisle and, to a lesser degree, Berwick (Newcastle or Edinburgh would have been more suitable), this presented no great problems, and was a situation which had existed even in pregrouping days. There was however a distinct lack of regional co-operation, old feelings dying hard, and for a time the railways continued to be run virtually as before. Many services indeed had their origins dating back to World War I.

The desire to divide the country into strictly self-contained watertight areas and separate administrations does seem in many ways inappropriate for a railway network. It might have been of more primary importance to keep the main trunk routes under one control, and to retain these 'penetrating lines', as they were called, for operational purposes. No railway suffered more from these transfers than the former Midland, whose main line between Bristol and Leeds (now the most important of the 'Inter-City' routes not serving London) traversed four separate regions, the Western, Midland, Eastern and North Eastern. This must have made timetable planning at best an extremely complicated business. Similarly, the Midland route to Scotland traverses respectively the Midland, short of Sheffield, the Eastern to Skipton, then again back to the Midland, and finally the Scottish. Complications in the Birmingham area also gave rise to many problems of a similar nature.

Further regional boundary adjustments took place on 4 March 1957 in the north east and again on 1 February 1958, when former Southern Railway lines west of Exeter reverted from WR to SR, together with the transfer of the GWR Barnstaple branch to the Southern Region. The Plymouth area, however, remained under the control of the Western Region. Even more recently the SR main line between Salisbury and Exeter has been passed over to its old rival, the Western, which has proceeded to lower it to the status of an elongated secondary branch, reduced to single line, with all through trains to the west country beyond Exeter diverted to its own route via Taunton. The most recent adjustment at the time of writing is the merger of the Eastern and North Eastern Regions; the reason for the original separation of these was never very clear from the start.

Regarding British interests in Ireland, on nationalisation these passed to the London Midland Region of the Railway Executive. The lines of the old Belfast & Northern Counties Railway, acquired by the Midland Railway in 1903 under the title of the Midland Railway Northern Counties Committee, and in turn LMS/NCC, together with the narrow-gauge line between Londonderry and Strabane (in effect worked by the County Donegal Railway), became part of the newly formed Ulster Transport Authority as from 10 August 1948. In 1950 the British Transport Commission announced that it could not finance the Dundalk Newry & Greenore Railway (originally owned by the LNWR) after 31 December 1951, and this line finally ceased operation in 1953. This left only the County Donegal Railways Joint Committee, with the rather curious pre-1923 joint ownership of Midland Railway of England and Great Northern Railway of Ireland. By 1953 these concerns had become the British Transport Commission (London Midland Region) and the Great Northern of Ireland Board, which bodies continued to appoint their representatives to the Joint Commission. On the final closure in 1959 this country's interest in the Irish railways came to a conclusion. It may however be added that the Joint Committee continued to administer its bus and lorry services until 1 January 1971, when these were transferred to Coras Iompair Eireann, the Southern Ireland transport organisation.

Very soon after the establishment of the British Transport Commission in 1948, a committee had been appointed specially to prepare a report in conjunction with the Railway and London Transport Executives' proposals for improvement of rail passenger transport in the London area. This Railway (London Plan) Committee made its report on 1 February 1949. The main recommendations included the construction of a number of new tubes in central London, none of which has materialised except the new Victoria line which was in part anticipated. Some of them were to be of 17ft diameter, capable of taking full size stock from the main line railways. Electrification of most of the main suburban line railways north of the Thames, with the exception of the Great Western, was also recommended. Some of these schemes have since been implemented, but others such as the Great Northern and Midland lines, have not.* These services were to run, not into the termini of Kings Cross and St Pancras, but into deep-level tubes at Finsbury Park and West Hampstead. The Great Northern scheme even included the Alexandra Palace branch (this had already been planned before the war), but in the event this line was eventually closed entirely. The London & North Western suburban services were to be electrified from Tring, but not into Euston, a new loop on to the Great Central (also to be electrified) between Kenton and Preston Road giving access to Marylebone.

One of the earliest visible results of nationalisation was the repainting of trains and locomotives. The last received the first attention of all, and as early as 30 January 1948 there was an exhibition at Addison Road, Kensington, of four engines—all LMS class 5's—painted in four possible choices of livery (fully lined out on the left hand side only, adjacent to the platform from which they would be officially inspected). The range was not very wide or inspiring, including no less than three shades of green, which had been adopted by the LNER, GWR and SR, while the fourth was just black with a style of lining out which was nothing more or less than a pure reversion to the old LNWR dating back to the days of F. W. Webb. At this stage LMS red, which in many ways would have been the most suitable, was not even considered. There were one or two subsequent experiments with a very light green livery, given to a rebuilt 'Patriot' and a GWR 'Castle', but these were never followed up, although an LMS feature which was adopted was the smokebox door number plate, dating back to the old Midland days, clear and easily visible from the front end. Crewe, as twenty-five years earlier, refused to conform so far as LNWR engines were concerned.

The decision was finally made in favour of lined out black for mixed traffic types (plain black without embellishment for freight locomotives and most tank classes) and Great Western green for express engines. The adoption of the former LNWR livery turned the tables against this company's old rival,

the Midland, after the events of twenty-five years earlier at the grouping. Crewe had then been most indignant at the idea of painting its engines in Midland livery, and in fact refused to conform to any extent. Apart from the 'Claughtons', most locomotives continued to be turned out in black which had always been good enough for them. Now it was indeed a case of retribution, and the proud compounds and other passenger classes suffered the crowning indignity of having to appear in former LNWR guise. At first the words 'British Railways' appeared in full on the tender and tank sides, but this was soon to be superseded by the well known and perhaps notorious lion of which emblem a modified version appeared in 1957. A later decision was for an entirely new blue livery for the top link engines, and very odd some of these looked, GWR 'Kings' in particular, but this did not last very long. A very welcome brief return to LMS red was made in 1959 when twenty of the 'Coronation' Pacifics, 'Duchess' Pacifics, and four selected 'Princess' engines on the Liverpool run once more appeared in their rightful livery, more suitable and natural, which they retained until the end of their existence.

All these varieties of raiment resulted in some locomotives changing their colour almost after the manner of a chameleon. LMS Pacific No 46221 *Queen Elizabeth*, for instance, started life in 1937 with the streamlined 'Coronation' in the then newly introduced blue for this particular service, subsequently changing to Midland red, and later to wartime black. Under British Railways ownership it acquired respectively the new blue livery introduced in 1949, a short lived experiment which was abandoned in favour of Great Western green, and finally ended up once more in maroon, a slightly darker shade of Midland red, in common with others of the class as just mentioned.

The LMS maroon was perpetuated for many years on coaching stock after an initial and rather unfortunate experiment with a two-toned livery, light red with cream upper panels, not unattractive but never achieving popularity. There was also a trial with the old LNWR livery—plum and spilt milk was now the official description—and for a number of years the Western Region main line stock was repainted in the old GWR livery of chocolate and cream. The Southern too retained its plain unlined green for all its passenger coaches, this colour also being applied on all regions to electric multiple units. To conclude the livery story, even if it means looking ahead somewhat, diesel railcars, when they appeared on

*Authorisation of the electrification of the GNR outer suburban lines was announced just before going into print.

the scene, were dark green with a yellow waistband, but the first diesel locomotives, also green, were un-lined, giving them a somewhat plain if not drab appearance. Later however, variations on some classes resulted in a much more attractive two-tone livery of light and dark shades of green separated by a yellow band. The Western Region also experimented with maroon, unfortunately unlined, and also a self explanatory colour called desert sand. All of these were swept away with the complete change started in 1964 to universal blue for everything, even including diesel shunters, main-line coaching stock having white upper panels, the result being extremely cold and clinical. So much uniformity has, it must be admitted, become more than a little overpowering and monotonous, and one often wishes for a little relief, even if only in the form of some sort of lining out. A red waistband, for instance, would form a pleasant contrast, now only provided by the ugly yellow front ends, deliberately startling of course to perform the very desirable function of providing strong visual impact for the safety of men working on the line.

British Railways inherited a total of 20,445 loco-motives at its inception in 1948 from the four rail-ways, and it was immediately obvious that a unified numbering system would have to be adopted to avoid confusion. For a short period the easy exped-ient of prefixing the number by the letters M, E, W, and S was followed. This was a case of railway history repeating itself, for twenty-five years earlier the then newly formed LNER and SR had adopted a similar system, only to abandon it in favour of the simple process of adding an appropriate number of thousands to the old numbers. This latter method was now again applied, although Great Western engines were unaltered. This railway, alone of the four, still retained cast metal plates which could not be amended whereas the other three had long adopt-ed painted numerals. Thus the Southern engines simply added 30000 to their old numbers, the LMS 40000 (as they already had a large number of eng-ines above 9999 this resulted in many engines appearing in the 50000s), while the LNER added 60000. The 10000s were allocated to diesel locomo-tives, and the 20000s to electric. Incidentally it may be mentioned that the LNER had already in 1946 carried out a complete renumbering of its locomo-tives on a logical basis, with all classes and wheel specifications grouped together in one block, in place of the previous system which had perpetuated the numbers acquired in pre-grouping days.

The same situation arose with coaching stock, but in this case the letter system was adopted perman-ently, and there was never any attempt at a com-plete renumbering scheme. Coaches were allocated to particular regions, this being indicated by a letter prefix (in addition to the suffix denoting origin), so that a prenationalisation coach would bear a number such as Sc3529E—a former North British, late LNER vehicle, with the Sc indicating its regional allocation (S on its own was borne by Southern Region stock). Newly constructed BR designs of coaches carried the regional prefix, but of course no suffix. In the early 1960s an attempt was made to separate the allocation of coaching stock employed in East Anglia by the adoption of the prefix GE, revival of the pre-grouping title of Great Eastern, but this did not last long. More recently a similar idea was introduced in the north east and inaugur-ated with the appearance of the letters NE on some coaching stock, but this again vanished when the North Eastern Region was abolished and merged into the Eastern Region.

A range of standard coaches of new design for various duties began to appear in 1950. By 1954 over 2,000 had been built, of seventeen types, all of them except for the non-corridor fitted with auto-matic buckeye couplings, which had been standard-ised. Pre-nationalisation coaches are almost entirely extinct, and even many of the earlier BR ones have already disappeared. Wooden bodied coaches, still commonly encountered even on the main lines in 1948, are no longer to be seen. Six-wheelers were already becoming scarce, and the last in use on any of the former main lines were probably some Great Eastern specimens, which were still to be found on the Laxfield branch, the old Mid-Suffolk Light Rail-way, until the end of 1951 (the line was closed in 1952).

The spartan wooden seat without upholstery of Victorian trains had of course long been consigned to limbo, possibly the last examples in ordinary service being the old North London four-wheelers, some of which survived to the early 1930s, although occasionally even in recent years specimens were to be found on colliery workman's trains in out-of-the-way corners of the country. All the more surprising, therefore, when it again became possible to ride in a wooden seated passenger coach, and on a main line at that! In 1949 the ever enterprising and original Mr Bulleid built at Eastleigh eight buffet cars modelled on the lines of the good old English pub and bearing such appropriate names as the

Green Man, Jolly Tar, and so on, part of the exteriors being painted in a mock imitation of old-fashioned brickwork. The interior was designed as far as possible to resemble a saloon bar, but they never became very popular, mainly owing to the complete absence of windows; one could not view the passing scenery, nor be quite sure where you were. This was perhaps carrying the idea of the mock-up interior decoration a little too far, and they were eventually rebuilt on more conventional lines.

The life expectation of rolling stock seems to have decreased considerably in recent years. In 1948, for instance, 12,000 coaching vehicles, 21.5% of the whole, were over thirty-five years old. Standards of comfort have probably in general greatly improved, although it cannot but be regretted that since 1962 no side corridor vehicles have been built for what are now known as second class passengers (the change of designation from what had been previously known as third class was made on 3 June 1956). Centre gangway is now standard, eminently suitable for some sorts of duties such as excursion trains, and indeed apparently preferred by some passengers, but lacking in the privacy and peacefulness of the compartment, apart from the disadvantages of draughtiness owing to inconsiderate opening of windows and carelessness in closing communication doors. It is now only the privileged first class passenger who can be sure of absence from such disturbances. The decision was probably in the main influenced by the fact that it is more practical to accommodate four passengers a side in two pairs of seats separated by a central aisle than within the confines of a compartment. With the replacement by diesel railcars for most shorter distance services (and not always so short!) the old conception of the five-a-side non-corridor compartment coach, once so universal on local journeys, has almost vanished. It is to be found at the time of writing on some electrified suburban routes around London and Manchester, and on the old Great Northern residential services out of Kings Cross and Moorgate.

The Railway Executive, which as from 1 January 1948 became responsible for control of the main line railways, consisted of seven full-time members. The chairman was Sir Eustace Missenden, late general manager of the Southern, with Mr R. A. Riddles (vice-president of the LMS), Mr V. M. Barrington Ward (assistant general manager LNER), Mr D. Blee (goods manager GWR), Mr W. P. Allen, and General Sir William Slim, the last mentioned being the first instance of the appointment of a non-railway man for the direction of running such a concern as a railway, with all its requirements of specialised knowledge and experience. This somewhat curious practice has been adopted in other industries in more recent years, the ethics and advantages or otherwise of which would be a controversial subject outside the scope of this book. (One is reminded of the old saying 'A cobbler should stick to his last'.)

Mr Riddles, who as recorded in the previous chapter, had been responsible for the design of the WD 2–8–0 and 2–10–0 engines during the war, now became with Mr R. C. Bond as his principal assistant, the first CME of British Railways. As it was to turn out, he was the last one, so far as steam traction—of which he was a staunch advocate—was concerned. On Mr Riddles' retirement, Mr Bond became CME, BR Central Staff, and he in turn became Technical Adviser on 1 October 1958, to be succeeded by Mr J. F. Harrison (then occupying the position of Chief Mechanical and Electrical Engineer, LMR). This post controlled both the Mechanical and Carriage and Wagon Departments of BR. Mr Harrison was in turn succeeded by Mr A. E. Robson as CMEE of the London Midland Region.

For the moment, whatever the long term consideration of the future might be, the immediate necessity was for the construction of large numbers of new locomotives to replace many of the existing fleet of 20,445 engines inherited from the four main line railways, a considerable number of them of pre-grouping types which would already have become extinct but for the exigencies of the war. Already there were quite a number of orders of pre-nationalisation types in hand, the construction of which would continue until at least 1951 (one GWR design actually as late as 1956, as already mentioned). Most intriguing and unique was the perpetuation, not only of a pre-nationalisation, but actually a pre-grouping design dating back to 1898. This was the construction between 1949 and 1951 of twenty-eight North Eastern 0–6–0Ts identical with the original engines first introduced by Wilson Worsdell and later multiplied by successive CMEs, the last having been built by Gresley in 1925.

An early decision which had to be made by the new body was concerning the types for the future. One important consideration was that they should be of simple and robust design with no unnecessary complications and easy to maintain, as it was foreseen that it would be a long time if ever (as indeed it turned out) before pre-war standards of upkeep could return. To a certain extent engines had to be designed to look after themselves. This meant that Mr Bulleid's Pacifics, good though they were in many respects, could not be considered as likely candidates for their adoption as a standard type top link express engine. GWR designs were ruled out owing to their restricted route availability, the overall cylinder width exceeding platform and other clearances on many of the other railway lines. Gresley's three cylinder types had shown themselves during the war to be at a severe disadvantage under conditions of poor maintenance, while the engines of his successors, Thompson and Peppercorn, were comparative newcomers. Nevertheless an extensive series of trials between representative classes of all four groups was undertaken during 1948 over one another's lines, as far as possible under identical conditions, before any final decision was taken. The fact that Riddles was an LMS man, and the considerations already enumerated, made it not surprising that some of that company's designs were finally adopted, with some modifications, as the basis of certain of the twelve standard types which were eventually evolved. For a full and comprehensive account, written with inside knowledge, the reader must be referred to 'British Railways Standard Steam Locomotives' by Mr E. S. Cox.

One of the first steps taken to explore the possible benefits of the transfer of some types of existing locomotives to other than their native systems, was the despatch of two newly built LMS 2-6-4Ts, Nos 42198 and 42199, on 14 April 1948 to the Southern Region. They were tried out principally from Tunbridge Wells on the Oxted line services and the other outer suburban services still not electrified or scheduled for conversion to electric working. Something new was needed to replace the ageing LBSC I3 tanks and other types, and the new 2-6-4Ts showed themselves to be ideally suited, with the result that further engines of the type were built at Brighton specially for the Southern Region.

Similar forms of integration were to follow in other parts of the country, such as Ivatt lightweight 2-6-0s for the Cambrian lines. At various periods of exceptional circumstances, such as shortage of motive power in some areas, interesting temporary transfers took place, as instanced by the appearance of LNER Green Arrows on the Bournemouth line in 1953 and unrebuilt West Countries on the Great Eastern in 1951. The Gresley Garratt No 69999,

rendered superfluous on its banking duties on the Worsboro' incline by electrification, was transferred to similar duties on the Lickey, but here it never gained the popularity with the drivers at Bromsgrove of the Midland 0-10-0 *Big Bertha*.

The headquarters of the new Railway Executive was at first temporarily located at 55 Broadway, Westminster, already occupied by London Transport, but in October 1947 moved to 222 Marylebone Road. Here Mr R. A. Riddles, now Chief Mechanical Engineer, made several appointments to deal with matters directly under his jurisdiction, among whom may be noted Mr R. C. Bond, responsible for locomotives and maintenance, and Mr E. S. Cox, already referred to, who as executive officer, design, had in effect much to do with the actual planning and construction of the new standard types.

Mr Cox, like Mr Riddles, was an LMS man, having served his apprenticeship on the old Lancashire & Yorkshire, and already had considerable experience in the locomotive departments of that railway and the LMS. It was hardly surprising therefore that the new designs would bear the hallmark of LMS practice, at the same time incorporating some of Mr Cox's own ideas, such as the provision of two outside cylinders and high running plates to give maximum accessibility. He was definitely not a 'splasher' man. The modest 'maxi', to put it into more modern terms, had already started to disappear as long ago as 1914 on the old LSWR with Urie's 4-6-0s. These were in complete contrast to their immediate predecessor, the last batch of Drummond 4-6-0s of 1911/2, which with their voluminous skirts were purely Edwardian. In between the two extremes, the still respectable 'midi' remained for many years at varying heights, always trying to get shorter and higher, but managing to retain respectability so far as highly bred passenger engines were concerned. One must ignore in this connection the monstrosities built mainly for conversion from broad to standard gauge which appeared on the Great Western in the Victorian era. What may be termed the lower classes, the freight and shunting engines, never aspired to the same standards of modesty, and their much smaller wheels did not in any case make for such a leggy appearance. It was not until 1926, with the appearance of the Horwich 2-6-0s, that the ultimate 'mini', which would have been considered the height of indecency in Edwardian days, had now to be accepted, and became commonplace on such designs as the Stanier 'black 5'. It still did not quite

23

reach its ultimate until the Bulleid wartime Q1 0–6–0s and, at the end of 1947, the Ivatt class 4 2–6–0s with their complete absence of running plates. This last was one of the types which formed the basis of one of the twelve new BR standard designs of Mr Cox. Others such as the class 5 4–6–0, 2–6–4T, and lightweight 2–6–0 and 2–6–2Ts, also showed their obvious ancestry, but the Britannias, the first class to appear, were quite new in conception.

The last design of all, the splendid class 9 2–10–0s of 1957, of which 251 examples were built, was also quite individual and was probably the finest of all the standard types. Although intended primarily for freight work, they did on occasion appear on express passenger trains, on which they are recorded as having attained ninety mph, but such speeds with ten coupled five foot driving wheels were quickly frowned on by the authorities. It was absolutely tragic that such magnificent machines were destined to have such short lives, consequent on the abandonment of steam. It is perhaps not too much to say that if this event had not come about with such complete and inexcusable haste, there would have been every likelihood that Mr Cox might have realised what must have been a life long ambition, to attain the post of chief mechanical engineer. One can only sympathise with him that this was just one of those unfortunate things which was destined not to be.

Space does not permit more than a brief reference to sundry experimental variations from standard applied to some of the new engines, notably the fitting of Franco Crosti boilers to ten of the 2–10–0s, Caprotti valve gear on thirty of the class 5s (and also on the one and only three cylinder Pacific *Duke of Gloucester*, never multiplied owing to the onset of dieselisation), mechanical stokers, roller bearings, and so on. All of these are fully described in Mr Cox's book already referred to. Mention may however be made of the Giesl ejector, a modified form of blast pipe, which on some European railways had been shown to result in considerable economies in coal consumption. British Railways however showed a surprising lack of interest and it was tried out on only two engines, a Bulleid SR Pacific and one of the class 9 2–10–0s. This last was indeed a very odd and unsuitable choice, as Dr Giesl's invention had comparatively small scope for improving on the thermal efficiency of an already very fine design, one of the best this country had ever produced and a fitting climax to the history of

the British steam locomotive. The Giesl ejector would undoubtedly have shown up to much better advantage if it had been applied to an older design, such as an original Gresley Pacific, a mixed traffic 4–6–0, or even something like a Midland class 4 goods or Great Western pannier tank. The comparatively small cost of fitting would have been more than compensated by the saving in coal consumption, even though the engines had only a few years to run. By this time however any expenditure to improve the efficiency of the steam locomotive was not, on the grounds of policy, to be considered.

Before leaving the subject of locomotives as a whole one must refer again to that original and controversial character Mr O. V. Bulleid. His war time Pacifics have already received mention in an earlier chapter. In 1947 however the Southern Railway had authorised the construction of five engines of a revolutionary design, a 0–6–6–0 single boiler articulated with many unusual features, such as a cab at either end with duplicate controls to avoid the necessity of turning. This meant, among other things, that the poor fireman had to work alongside the boiler amidships under almost impossible conditions. It really ought to have been designed as an oil burner. It was intended for general mixed traffic use, and may perhaps be regarded as a last valiant effort to maintain steam propulsion against the advance of electrification, and still more the growing threat of the diesel, which had hardly yet got more than a slight foothold in this country but was already well established in America. The initial teething troubles were many. Bulleid himself could probably have made something of the project, given time and indulgent co-operation, but after his departure the Railway Executive viewed it without enthusiasm. Of the three actually constructed only one was ever steamed and all of them very soon quietly faded away. Mr Bulleid duly departed to Ireland, to take over a similar position with the CIE, and even there pursued his idea for a similar machine, but built to burn turf in order to overcome the chronic coal shortage. Unfortunately this also never got beyond the trial stage.

Reverting to this country, steam was still the predominant motive power, and there seemed no early prospect of this being otherwise. The diesel had hardly begun to rear its ugly head except for purely shunting duties, in which sphere it had become fully established. It was significant that the twelve new standard steam types did not include any engines for such work. Such developments as could be more readily anticipated at this stage lay in the sphere of electrification. So far as main lines were concerned the only important conversion—apart from certain outer suburban services on the Southern, such as Brighton, Eastbourne, and Portsmouth, which hardly qualified for the description of main lines in the widest sense—had been the Manchester-Sheffield and Wath line, completed in 1954, which carried a heavy freight traffic. This was on the 1,500 volt overhead system, as was the LNER's other scheme, the suburban lines out of Liverpool Street to Shenfield and Southend. These were converted to 6·25kv and 25v AC during the weekend of 4-7 November 1960. The 1,500 volt DC system had been recommended as long ago as 1931 by the Weir report as a standard for future electrification, but was not taken up by the Southern, which adhered to its third rail 750 volts, in many ways quite unsuitable for main line working. As a result the southern counties must now inevitably remain a separate entity from whatever future electrification extensions may occur in the rest of the country. This was recognised even in 1951 when a committee appointed by the Railway Executive produced a report regarding the future policy in this sphere. So far as the Southern Region was concerned, it recommended a boundary of third rail electrification east and south of Weymouth, Salisbury and Reading, which is very largely what has occurred since.

This 1951 report consisted of a ninety-four page booklet issued by the British Transport Commission, which also included a number of maps. It is not possible here to do other than to briefly summarise the general conclusions reached. The most important was that outside the area within the Southern Region already referred to, and the London Transport system, where 750 volts should remain standard, all further schemes should be with the direct current overhead line at 1,500 volts DC (already recommended by the Weir report of twenty years earlier), but that application might be made to use a voltage of 3,000 in special circumstances. However, initial experiments were carried out in 1952 on the small isolated line between Lancaster and Heysham, originally converted to electric traction by the Midland Railway in 1908. As a result of these trials it was recommended that future main line electrification should employ 25kv 50 cycle AC with overhead conductors taking current from the national grid system.

Some interesting statistics were contained in this report:

As at 31 December 1949, mileage of main line railways and London Transport Executive:

Route miles not electrified	18,635
Electrified or work in progress	1,193

(includes 191 miles of London Transport lines)

Motive Power

Steam locomotives	19,790

(Note that this total had already been reduced from 20,445 as at 1 January 1948)

Electric locomotives in use and under construction	117
Diesel electric locomotives	100
Passenger coaches (locomotive hauled)	51,690
Passenger coaches (electric multiple unit)	8,547

The diesel multiple unit, it will be observed, had not yet appeared on the scene, apart from one or two pre-war experiments by the GWR and LMS.

In this same year, 1951, the Conservative Party, which had been against nationalisation from the start, once again came into power, and announced a policy of decentralisation of the railway administration, now controlled centrally from 222 Marylebone Road (sometimes irreverently referred to in some quarters as 'the Kremlin'). This resulted in a further Transport Bill which became law on 6 May 1953. Under it the Railway Executives (apart from the London Transport Executive) were abolished as from 30 September 1953. Each Region now had its own chief regional manager, with increased powers, who was responsible direct to the Commission. The original Act of 1947 had stipulated that BTC must pay its way 'taking one year with another', however that might have been intended to be interpreted. By 1952 wages had already risen by 30% since 1948, and some essential major railway commodities by very serious amounts indeed, as for instance 275% for coal, 330% for steel rails, 430% for copper plates and 450% for timber sleepers. Nevertheless, by considerable economies and increase in charges, passenger fares now being 90% above pre-war and goods rates 150%, a small surplus of receipts over working expenditure had been achieved for each of the years, although not enough to cover the standing charges such as fixed interest on the government stock, the amount of which had risen from £1,150 million in December 1948 to £1,440 million in 1952.

In 1954 there took place in Britain, for the third time since its establishment in 1885, the meeting of the International Railway Association Congress. The previous occasions had been in 1895 and 1925, very appropriately the year which also celebrated

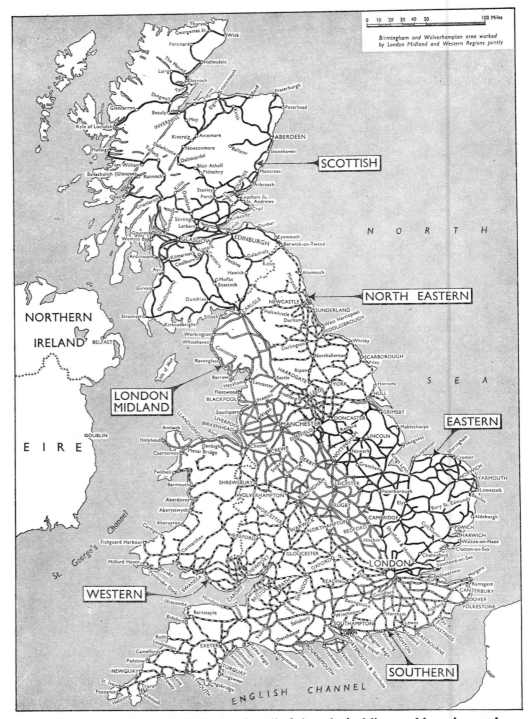

The railway map as it was in 1954, showing all of the principal lines and branches, and the composition of the six regions at that time, and before the wholesale closures which have since taken place.

the centenary of the opening of the Stockton & Darlington Railway. In many ways the conditions as regards the railways of this country bore strong resemblance to those of twenty-nine years before. At both periods the railways were in a state of major re-organisation, the first time coming within two years of the grouping while on this occasion they were still undergoing the upheavals of nationalisation.

The deliberations of the Congress, so far as it affected the railways of this country, covered a wide range of subjects, such as locomotive standardisation—already referred to—the prospects of future electrification, adoption of diesel or gas turbine traction (the latter was already being tried out on the Western Region), progress in civil engineering including the wider adoption of flat bottom rails, concrete sleepers and pre-fabricated track laying, signalling (colour light signals, for instance, increased from 3,000 in 1939 to 7,000 in 1953), general increased mechanisation, use of road-rail containers, the hotel and catering services, relations between staff and management and, rather ominously, the closure of unremunerative branch lines. Already, since 1948, over two hundred of these, comprising some 1,500 route miles, had lost their passenger services, although most of these were continuing with freight traffic, and another three hundred stations had been closed to passengers both on main and branch lines. This subject must inevitably come up again when we come to the Beeching era.

The question of safety on railways in this country was also touched upon, it being pointed out that by a very wide margin rail was still by far the safest form of travel. Passenger fatalities during the period 1946-1952 were one for every thirty-five million passenger journeys, and one for every 544 million passenger miles, which means that the chance of losing one's life in a railway accident is so remote as to be in practice negligible. How your author came within an ace of being one of these one-in-several-million exceptions he may perhaps be forgiven for recounting in a moment. The record of the railways of this country with the number of serious accidents since the close of World War II is probably the lowest of any similar comparable period of the last hundred years, but this is to some extent offset by the fact that it includes two out of the three most disastrous, from the point of view of the number of casualties, in the whole history of the railways of the British Isles. These were Harrow on 8 October 1952 and Lewisham on 4 December 1957. They

had one feature in common, in that the direct cause in each case was the passing of a signal at danger in conditions of poor visibility, amounting in the case of Lewisham to thick fog.

The Harrow accident involved the 7.31 am local train from Tring to Euston, which was a very popular one on which the author frequently travelled. Its normal formation was a standard seven coach non-corridor set with two additional coaches at the rear; on this occasion a couple of pre-grouping thirds of L & YR and Midland origin. By the merest chance I happened not to be on the train on this particular day, but I invariably travelled on one of these last two coaches which bore the worst brunt of the accident by being ploughed into by the following express. There were no survivors in them, and my narrow escape I have only been able to regard as providential. My guardian angel must have been working overtime that day! It was normal practice to divert the train from the up slow to the up fast line at the crossover just north of Harrow, to give it a clear run into Euston, the twelve miles non-stop frequently occupying only fourteen or fifteen minutes. I had on occasion known it to cover the distance in almost even time, by as mere a margin as really makes no difference. This must have been very rare for a similar distance on any suburban train over any line in the London area. The engine was always a 2–6–4T from Watford shed, working bunker first, the two favourites being one of the earlier Fowler engines stationed there, Nos 42304 and 42389, the latter being the one on that fateful day. No damage occurred to the engine at the front end of the train; indeed, some passengers were unaware that anything unusual had happened.

The train had just started to leave for its smart run up to Euston, when it was run into at the rear by the up Perth (8.15 pm the previous evening) express with engine 46242. This in itself would have been bad enough, but almost immediately, before anything could be done, the wreckage was ploughed into by the 8.00 am Euston-Liverpool, double headed by *Jubilee* No 45637 and Pacific No 46202 *Princess Anne*, only recently rebuilt from the experimental turbine locomotive. It thus only had a few weeks of life in its converted state for both of these engines were damaged beyond repair. In the resulting carnage ninety-eight passengers and four of the enginemen on the footplate of the two expresses lost their lives. Another ten died later in hospital, the resulting toll of 112 fatalities being exceeded in the history of this country only by the

Gretna accident of 1915, in which 227 persons were killed. This also was a double collision including two passenger trains. In the case of Harrow there were of course three.

The cause of the Lewisham disaster, which occurred in thick fog, must be attributed to the driver of the *West Country* Pacific running at far too high a speed in the prevailing conditions of thick fog, something like the 'motorway madness' which occurs only too frequently in these days. As a result he passed two colour light signals at danger, possibly because of partial obscurity due to drifting steam over the cab, a trouble to which this class and many others were particularly prone. The engine ran into the back of a crowded electric train, the resulting toll being eighty-eight killed. At nearby Hither Green another serious accident occurred on 5 November 1967, claiming forty-nine victims. This time a diesel electric multiple unit from Hastings was involved, the cause being derailment at high speed owing to a broken rail.

Another accident of rather more than usual interest to the author occurred at Bourne End, only two miles from his home, a general cross-over between the fast and slow lines which at this time existed between Berkhamsted and Boxmoor on the old LNWR main line. It was early on a Sunday morning, on 30 September 1945, when I casually observed from my window the passing of the up Perth overnight express hauled by unrebuilt *Royal Scot* No 6157. An ordinary enough event, it was not until several hours later that I learned it had come to grief only a couple of minutes afterwards. The actual circumstances were simple enough; it took the cross-over from fast to slow line at high speed instead of observing the necessary twenty mph restriction. This unaccountable lapse of an experienced driver, who regrettably lost his life, was never satisfactorily explained. One possible solution may be that the rising run, on this bright morning, happened to be directly ahead of forward vision at this point, and blinded the driver's view of the colour light distant signal, the purpose of which was to give warning of the approach to Bourne End crossing and which in view of the diversion would have stood at danger. The engine negotiated the first switch over to the slow line, but failed to take the second, and rolled over on its side down the embankment taking some coaches with it. It lay there for three weeks before it was possible to raise it. The death toll was forty-three.

Finally, one must refer to a more recent occurrence at Hixon, on the old North Stafford line between Colwich and Stone, on 6 January 1968, which highlighted the potential dangers of the modern unmanned half barrier level crossing. A Manchester-London express came into collision with a lorry low-loader conveying a transformer which had become stuck in the crossing. Three men in the driving cab of the electric locomotive lost their lives, together with eight passengers. This accident stressed the need for the revision of the rules and regulations regarding the operation of these barriers, and while the necessary modifications were being carried out the installation of new crossings of this type was held in abeyance.*

*For full report of this accident and many others, readers are referred to an excellent book 'Railway Accidents of Great Britain and Europe' produced by the present publishers in 1970.

Modernisation

The announcement made by Sir Brian Robertson, then chairman of the BTC, on 25 January 1955, of plans for the complete modernisation of the railway system was as unexpected in its far reaching implications as could be imagined. The need for some drastic innovations had been becoming increasingly apparent to meet the challenge of road, and now, on a widening scale, air competition. It was, however, the startling decision to plan towards the complete abandonment of steam motive power that provided the main bombshell, because it was a sudden and complete change of policy which occurred almost overnight. As recently as 1951, Colonel Rudgard, chief of motive power, in referring to diesel electric propulsion as a possible rival to steam, had stressed that the simplicity, reliability and, above all, the comparatively low initial cost, made steam still the most efficient and economical source of rail motive power for the country's needs. From the point of view of actual economies it had been stated that the use of diesel locomotives with their high initial cost could only be justified when they could be in continual twenty-four hour use, and the opportunities of providing practicable rota schedules were in this country extremely limited. This was now conveniently forgotten. The underlying explanation for this sudden volte face, whether political, or whether prompted by vested interests, oil or whatever, has never been satisfactorily explained. The whole matter however seemed somehow to have a rather unsavoury smell of an unholy alliance of big business and politics.

An initial estimate of the period in which steam would gradually be phased out was about twenty to twenty-five years, that is somewhere between 1975 and 1980. Had it been suggested that the 250 steam locomotives yet to be built, and the entire existing fleet of nearly 18,000 would have been eliminated within a period of thirteen years, it would have been regarded as so fantastic as to be unbelievable. Yet this is what actually happened. The steam locomotive, after a reign of a century and a quarter, was already on the decline. It seems in the light of more recent experiences destined eventually to be entirely superseded by other forms of motive power, although it will be many years before this happens in some parts of the world, notably India. So far as this country is concerned, it was the grossly indecent haste with which the operation was carried out that was so completely unjustified. The average life of a steam engine is anything from thirty years upwards, very often much more, and the wanton destruction of so much fine machinery after only a very few years of use was an appalling and disgraceful waste which should never have been countenanced.

It must be readily conceded that under the modern desire for ever more speed, steam propulsion could not have answered today's demands for schedules such as are now to be found on the electrified lines to Manchester and Liverpool, at any rate within the limits of the British loading gauge. The same applies to some of the more recent accelerated timings on the East Coast route and the Western Region, with diesel haulage, but there were and are still plenty of secondary and goods services which could have been very well maintained by steam locomotives working out at least some of their unexpired life on economic grounds alone. Specific areas such as South Wales, with its coal supplies, would have been particularly suitable. The question of coal emphasises the folly of a country with ample coal resources committing itself to be dependent entirely on fuel supplies from overseas.

Electrification is a far more logical proposition, and ought to have been applied on a very much wider scale. Even after the success of the London to Manchester and Liverpool scheme it hung fire for too long, and it is perhaps fortunate that the unexplained delay in the obvious extension to Scotland was at a late hour sanctioned by the Labour Government in its last months of office. Whether the Conservatives, noticeably less sympathetic to rail transport, would have acted likewise is conjectural. It is to be hoped, however, that further major electrification schemes will follow. The East Coast line to Leeds and Newcastle cries out for it, as does some of the Western Region, particularly Paddington-Bristol, and perhaps Cardiff and Swansea, with an obvious link-up between Bristol, Birmingham, Sheffield and Leeds, now the most important main line in the country away from London. Completion of the Midland main line to Leicester, Nottingham and Sheffield would link up most of the important towns and cities in the country. These could all be implemented at a fraction of the enormous sums now being spent annually on the construction of new motorways.

Electrification schemes on a smaller scale were in fact inaugurated during the latter part of the 1950s and 1960s: the Colchester-Clacton-Southend lines of the LNER together with the former LT & SR Southend lines, the suburban lines in the Glasgow area, and the Southern Kent Coast extension embracing all lines of the former SE & CR with the exception of the Hastings route. The reason given for the omission of the latter was the curious one that special narrow stock would have to be provided in view of the limited clearance of Bo-peep tunnel, St Leonards (as it always had in steam days) and this could not be worked in with the other services. The oddness of this contention was that narrow diesel multiple units were used in lieu, and thus special narrow trains had in any event to be provided for this route.

Even before the announcement of the 1955 modernisation plan, diesel multiple units had begun to make their appearance, the first being put into service in 1954 between Leeds and Bradford and on the old Maryport & Carlisle Railway, followed by some parts of the north east and East Anglia and also the Birmingham area. Eventually they spread all over the country except on the Southern, which introduced its own brand of diesel electric units for a few services. The standard type elsewhere was diesel mechanical with direct transmission, which eventually totalled some 4,600 coaches. These were of many varying types and formations, from two car or even single units to sets comprised of three or four coaches. These could be used in multiple to form longer trains for such duties as the suburban services out of St Pancras and Paddington, on which they were not too suitable, especially under conditions of overcrowding. There were also some semi main line sets designed for inter city express work, such as the *Trans Pennine Express* between Liverpool and Hull, and some so-called luxury all-Pullman trains for use on the Midland main line and the Western Region.

Eventually the diesel multiple units entirely displaced the old time steam hauled local stopping trains, and it is a pity that this change was accompanied by such a general deterioration in comfort. They were to some extent popular at first, particularly because of the clear look-out ahead which could be enjoyed by passengers in the front seats, but after the novelty had worn off and they began to get rough in riding, the combined disadvantage of noise, vibration, and smell became only too apparent. Experienced passengers endeavoured to secure a seat in the trailing vehicle away from the power bogies, because it must be said that to have to travel in one of these vehicles, particularly in run down condition, represents the very lowest form of life in rail transport. Even the electric multiple unit, for long notorious for its rough riding (although this problem has been largely overcome in more recent years), is at least comparatively quiet and entirely odourless. The DMU may be endurable for a comparatively shorter distance, but only too often there is a tendency to use these for lengthy journeys over main lines, and they can never pretend to attain the comfortable standard of a locomotive hauled train.

There was in 1955, when the modernisation plan was commenced, a modest total of six diesel electric main line locomotives, Nos 10000, 10001 and 10800 on the London Midland Region, and Nos 10201-10203 on the Southern. There was also an experimental 4-8-4 diesel mechanical No 10100 (withdrawn in 1958 after catching fire in Manchester Central station), and two gas turbines, Nos 18000 and 18100 on the Western. The Southern had three electric locomotives and the Eastern Region sixty-eight for use on its Manchester-Sheffield and Wath route, then the only full scale electrified main line in the country.

The initial order for new diesel locomotives was for 174 engines of ten types, and it was intended that these should receive extensive trials before deciding which were the most suitable for further construction. This was known as the pilot scheme, and the first of them No D8000, a Bo–Bo type 1000hp was delivered by English Electric on 3 June 1957, followed by the remainder of the initial order, together with the remaining types, during 1957-8. Unfortunately the authorities were in such a hurry to proceed with the dieselisation programme that they could not wait for the results of the projected trials, and several more designs were ordered in quantity straight off the drawing board, without any practical experience of their capabilities.

The subsequent sorry history of these early years of dieselisation is well known and cannot be gone into in detail here. It is sufficient to say that while some of the designs proved reasonably satisfactory, although all suffered from teething troubles, others were quite unsuitable from the start and gave endless trouble. Among these were some built by the North British Locomotive Company, with its splendid age-old reputation as builders of steam locomotives but with little or no experience of diesels. Regrettably this old established firm went out of business a few years later. In all these early designs there was one which was intended to be a new top link express class for the West Coast main line. This comprised ten I-Co-Co-I Sulzer engine units, Nos D1 to D10, known as the Peak class as they were given names after well known mountains, *Scafell Pike*, *Helvellyn*, *Snowdon*, and so on. They were found to be so unreliable that their sojourn at Camden was short, and they were transferred to Toton for freight work on which they have remained ever since. The design however was modified and the subsequent engines Nos D11-D193 were eminently satisfactory. They have become the mainstay of express services over the former Midland Railway.

By the end of 1959 there were 326 main line diesels in service, mostly diesel electric. Locally we had some very uncomplimentary nicknames for some of them. The English Electric D200 class, which became the principal engines on the main line of the old LNWR, were known as 'Long Pongs' in view of their length and odiferous properties. The Western Region, which in true GWR fashion had to be different, went in for hydraulic transmission in lieu of diesel electrics. The general fleet of shunters had by now increased to no less than 1,373, and had practically taken over all yard shunting and similar duties. These engines again were of some twenty different types of 0-4-0 and 0-6-0 wheel arrangement.

Another important locomotive was a large 3,300 hp engine built by English Electric on its own account and loaned to BR for extended trials in October 1955. Known as the *Deltic*, it was painted in blue lined out with white bands, somewhat reminiscent of the LMS Coronation Scot of pre-war days. It at first worked on the London-Liverpool trains, and later on the Eastern Region for several years, during which time it received sundry modifications and at least two or three new engines. It eventually formed the basic design for twenty-two new units for service between Kings Cross and Newcastle. The original was retired and now rests in no less a place than the Science Museum at South Kensington, in company with *Caerphilly Castle*, but looking strangely out of place in company with the ancient exhibits with which it is surrounded. Some unkind opponents of dieselisation remarked after its successors had been working for a few months from Kings Cross that it was a pity that there were not twenty-two other museums in the country where the new arrivals could be sent!

The failure rate of diesels in those earlier years was alarmingly high, and recourse to steam operation was widespread. The diesel electric is a complicated machine compared with a robust steam engine, with so much that may go wrong, and when it does it is usually complete failure. To put it in very simple words, it either will or won't go! The steam locomotive on the other hand rarely sits down on the job entirely and usually manages to stagger along somehow. I recollect an amusing incident about 1950 when the 9.55 pm from Euston failed at Harrow with vacuum ejector trouble, with the result that the train brakes could not be released other than by manual manipulation of each individual coach. Eventually this was decided upon, and we proceeded carefully at about ten mph, but goodness knows what rules and regulations were being broken—an unbraked passenger train on a busy main line! On arrival at Watford a fitter appeared from the shed with no other tool than a large sledge-hammer, a few hefty whacks from which soon put matters right. One can hardly imagine a temperamental diesel responding to such primitive treatment!

One of the most frequent causes of trouble, strangely enough, was with the oil-fired heating boilers supplying steam for the train, and many a cold journey had to be endured because the kettle refused to boil! It was not unknown to find a steam engine running double-headed between the diesel and the train merely to supply steam for heating purposes rather than to provide additional power. During the great freeze-up of January/February 1963 the position got to a very low ebb in many areas. In the London division of the LMR there were at one time only two or three of the considerable fleet of Sulzer D5000s, then largely employed on the suburban services, in use, the remainder being frozen up or unusable for various reasons. Recourse had to be made hurriedly to resuscitate some withdrawn steam engines from scrap sidings to maintain the services.

The 1955 modernisation scheme had stated that no further steam locomotives would be built after the completion of the 1956 programme. This was finalised, as is fairly well known, by the appearance of No 92220, appropriately named *Evening Star*, from Swindon Works in March 1960. By this time a large number of engines were already in store, never to run again: London Midland Region 298, Eastern 164, North Eastern 121, Scottish 379, Western 111, and Southern 21. The total in service was now down to 14,000, a figure which by the end of 1961 had sunk to 7,800. The first area to be completely dieselised was East Anglia as from 9 September 1962. Kent had already for the most part been electrified, the remaining gaps being operated by diesel traction. Elsewhere steam was to linger on in ever diminishing amounts, although completely banished on the newly electrified lines of the LMR. It was perhaps a little ironic that the South Western section of the SR, in earlier years the pioneer in electrification, was destined to be the last stronghold of main line steam working which survived until July 1967. The last remnants of steam lingered on in the northwest until August 1968.

One side effect of the modernisation plan has been the disappearance of the old time running shed. New maintenance depots of course had to be provided for the upkeep of diesel locomotives, but these needed only to be few in number and widely dispersed. Special depots merely for stabling were unnecessary as a diesel locomotive can be locked up and left where it is overnight; this is the usual practice with yard shunters. Main line locomotives only require a suitable siding at a convenient point for signing-on. Sometimes old steam locomotive sheds are used for this purpose, but more often these have been completely demolished together with old type coaling stages or more modern coaling plant, ash disposal plant and watering facilities (although even diesel engines require a certain amount of water, not only for engine cooling, but also in the case of passenger engines for steam heating). Undoubtedly this is one direction in which dieselisation has resulted in considerable economies with the elimination of the expensive upkeep of a running shed and the staff required—shed master, running foreman, fitters, lighters-up, and so on, and also clerical personnel, the number of which would depend on the size of the depot.

A more serious consequence from the employment aspect was the inevitable run-down of workshop capacity, owing to the reduced amount of maintenance. On 19 September 1962, the BTC put forward its plans for reorganisation, the total effect of which would involve the reduction of the labour force from 56,000 to 38,000. Although this would be spread over four or five years this could not be absorbed by natural wastage. The reaction of the National Union of Railwaymen was naturally hostile. Of the principal locomotive works, it was planned to close entirely Stratford, Ashford, Caerphilly, Wolverhampton, Gorton, Horwich, Darlington, Cowlairs and Inverurie, leaving only Crewe, Derby, Doncaster, Swindon, Eastleigh, St Rollox and Inverness (Cowlairs and St Rollox being combined into one). Carriage work would be concentrated on Wolverton, Derby, York and Eastleigh, with the consequent closure of Lancing, Swindon and Earlstown, and wagon building would be principally at Ashford, Temple Mills, Horwich, Shildon and Barassie.

By the end of 1962 the total number of diesel locomotives had risen to 3,683, and the steam fleet was down to 8,767. By 1965, for the first time, the diesel total of 4,811 outnumbered that of steam, 2,989, by a considerable margin. The scrapping of such large numbers of steam engines got beyond the capacity of the railway itself and large numbers were henceforth sold to outside contractors for breaking up. No single class, even BR standard designs, was now intact, and many well known modern designs were already extinct. A particularly notorious and really unjustifiable case of premature withdrawal was with regard to the Stanier Pacifics, about eighteen of which were still in good condition and continuing to give excellent service, too good, in fact, as it resulted in their final undoing. On 21 March 1964, for instance, there had been five special trains to Aintree for the Grand National, all steam hauled, by Nos 46245, 46239, 46228, 46251 and 46240. It seemed that the authorities were worried that at this late stage these engines were being called up far too often to replace failed diesels, to the detriment of the modernisation image as seen by the public. Orders were therefore given in September 1964 that all were to be withdrawn immediately, whatever their condition. Such are the lengths to which prejudice and propaganda can be carried! They could at least have been transferred elsewhere, and some of these engines would have been invaluable in the last months of steam, particularly between Crewe and Carlisle where there were still not enough diesels available to take over entirely. Some turns had to be rostered for steam; by this time the Britannias were the most powerful locomotives left and recourse often had to be made to a class 5 on a fourteen coach train, essentially a four cylinder Pacific job.

Meanwhile progress in electrification had been continuing, chiefly on the West Coast main line. The first stage, between Manchester and Crewe, was completed in September 1960, followed by Crewe-Liverpool in January 1962. Work proceeded southwards, and the last section, from Willesden to Euston, was first energised on 18 November 1965. All steam working south of Nuneaton had ceased on 26 September 1965, and full electric working began on 3 January 1966. Although all live steam was now officially banned 'under the wires', on 10 March 1967 one more steam engine was to be seen proceeding under its own power. Moreover, it was a class never before seen on the line—the restored LNER No 3442 *The Great Marquess* which ran up light for working a rail tour.

Modernisation during these years was not of course confined entirely to motive power. The most noticeable changes from the public aspect were the rebuilding of Euston and Birmingham New Street, together with other rather less spectacular reconstructions such as Coventry (all of these of course in conjunction with the electrification) and Leeds.

Euston was a major operation in that a completely new station was to emerge on the ruins of the old one, with which it has not the slightest resemblance. That this was carried out without any interruption to traffic, apart from the temporary diversion of some trains to St Pancras, Marylebone and Addison Road, and the transfer of parcels traffic to a temporary station at Kilburn, was a masterpiece of organisation. A regrettable feature which incurred much publicity at the time was the destruction of the famous Doric Arch and the lofty Great Hall with its magnificent panelled ceiling. Suggestions that the arch might be removed to a position nearer Euston Road were said to be impracticable, owing to lack of space, but the finished lay-out shows this to have been entirely wrong, and there is ample room where this historic monument could have still stood. Now, alas, it is too late.

What can one say of these two new ultra-modern stations? No doubt they are in keeping with this day and age, but it is difficult to approve of the claustrophobic low roofs of Birmingham New Street, with the resultant concentration of diesel fumes provided by about 50 per cent of the trains, even if suitable for electric working. As for Euston, quite frankly I loved the old station, with its numerous nooks and crannies and, to the stranger, sometimes difficult-to-find platforms. It was in practice three stations in one. I shall no doubt be probably rightly accused of sentimentality and of old-fashioned intolerance of the new ultra-modern. May I plead that as one of the older generation I do not take kindly nor accept readily the plea that because a thing is new it must necessarily be better than the old.

Some improvement schemes have not always been exploited to full advantage, and a great deal of money was wasted in the construction of a very large fly-over at Bletchley to enable freight trains from the Midlands to the Western Region at Oxford to avoid the necessity of crossing the increasingly busy and high speed running main line on the level. An expensive and somewhat short-sighted project, it has never carried its anticipated volume of traffic and is, even only a few years after construction, virtually disused.

Of far more use was the much needed widening of the old GNR main line to four tracks between Hadley Wood and Potters Bar, which involved not only the reconstruction of the stations, but also new tunnel bores. This bottleneck had long been an extreme operational nuisance when the two lines had to deal with all the expresses and local services, sandwiched in with heavy freight traffic. The latter is now greatly diminished owing to the diversion of much of it to the electrified LNWR line, but even so the widening is still invaluable for today's high speed trains.

Recent years have regrettably seen the closure of some of our finest stations in principal cities, such as Manchester Central and Glasgow St Enoch, each with its huge single-span arched roof. Glasgow has in fact lost two of its four central stations, trains from the north previously accommodated at Buchanan Street now being diverted to Queen Street. Similarly, Edinburgh is now served by only one main station, Waverley, following the closure of Princes Street. Nottingham and Birmingham are also the poorer with the disappearance of the fine centrally situated stations of Victoria and Snow Hill respectively.* Trains which formerly ran into Leeds Central are now diverted into the rebuilt City station, a pleasant reconstruction in the modern style, retaining some of the air of spaciousness over the platforms so sadly lacking at Euston and Birmingham.

*At the time of writing a skeleton morning and evening service still operates from Snow Hill's one remaining platform.

The Beeching Era

YET A FURTHER reorganisation took place in 1962, with the passing of a British Transport Act which received the Royal Assent on 1 August in that year. The British Transport Commission was dissolved and its functions were divided between several new boards, British Railways, London Transport, and a Transport Holding Company covering such ancillary activities as docks and inland waterways, shipping, hotels, sundry road interests, and so on. The new British Railways Board capital was reduced by writing off accumulated losses of £475 million, with £650 million put into a suspense account. The

Board was now entitled to fix its own charges and was no longer required to be a common carrier. For five years exchequer assistance up to £450 million would be available to meet revenue losses. London Transport would still be run separately by an independent public authority.

Meanwhile Sir Brian Robertson had resigned as chairman of the British Transport Commission on 1 June 1961, and the Minister of Transport appointed Dr Richard Beeching, technical director of Imperial Chemical Industries, to succeed him at a salary of £24,000, the figure he had already been receiving from ICI, compared with Sir Brian Robertson's comparatively modest £10,000. The appointment was the subject of considerable comment, not unmixed with many misgivings. It was felt in many circles that the choice should have fallen on a senior railway officer with full experience of the particular specialised knowledge of railway working and administration which one might have thought essential.

Dr Beeching had of course a brilliant record in his own particular spheres and in the world of finance, but hardly any particular experience of railways, or even transport in general, with their own individual problems. In one of his earlier speeches at Newark on 15 March 1962, he indicated how he appreciated the fact that countries all over the world were finding that under modern conditions railways, and indeed public transport in general, could no longer be entirely a self supporting financial prospect, and were having to receive some sort of state subsidy on social grounds. British Railways themselves had for the last few years been incurring a substantial annual loss, and on Dr Beeching now lay the onerous task of taking the matter in hand during the next five years, the length of his appointment, after which it was generally understood he would go back to ICI. He also had to recommend what steps could and must be taken.

Already on 10 March 1960, Mr Macmillan, then Prime Minister, speaking in the House of Commons, said: 'First the industry must be of a size and pattern suited to modern conditions and prospects. In particular, the railway system must be remodelled to meet current needs, and the modernisation plan must be adapted to this new shape.' This was of course several years after the inauguration of the modernisation plan already referred to, which was now well under way, but it was becoming very obvious that this plan was to fall far short of solving the railways' difficulties as a whole.

Dr Beeching's work in examining the financial position of the railways culminated in his famous report published by the Stationery Office on 27 March 1963. This shocked not only the railway world but the general public at large, which had been anticipating severe curtailment of the railway system but had certainly not expected anything nearly so drastic as was contained in the new proposals. These involved, briefly, the withdrawal by 1970 of passenger services from some 5,000 out of 17,800 route miles and closure of no less than 2,363 out of 4,709 stations and halts as well as 800 goods depots. The series of maps which accompanied the report clearly indicated the severity of the truncation of the system, leaving many large areas with sizeable towns, such as the whole of the north of Scotland beyond Inverness, and several parts of Wales and the West Country, completely without railways.

The proposals of course came in for some severe criticism in many quarters, particularly as would be expected from those likely to be most affected. This was not only the travelling community but also the railway staff, among whom inevitable reduction in numbers would be necessary. It was pointed out that every closure would have to be studied with great care before any final decision was taken, and the views of the Transport Users' Consultative Committees would have to be taken into account, but it turned out in practice that these were only too often largely ignored or overridden, and they had no actual powers in the matter. The final arbitrator at that time was the Minister of Transport, Mr Marples, who had already shown considerable bias in favour of replacement of rail traffic by road. Even he however had to agree that in some cases the ensuing hardship which would arise did not justify the closure, and that the lines must be kept open with some form of subsidy, more recently called a 'grant aid'.

It must be admitted that Dr Beeching had an impossible job from the start to 'make the railways pay'. This he intended to interpret far too literally, and he attempted to evaluate each branch line or service ignoring the fact that it formed part of a general network and should certainly not be considered in isolation from the rest of the system. Not only this, but some of the figures produced by the accountants were found to be, if not actually 'cooked', at the very least misleading. Nowhere was this more apparent than in the case of the Isle of Wight, where many of the dubious and questionable methods of costing were brought to light in a recently published book on the subject.* This revealed, among other things, that no account had been taken of the island's proportion of through bookings from the mainland, mainly Waterloo, which would represent an estimated probable 90% of the total traffic on a summer Saturday! Another similar case pointing to the complete unreliability of the figures produced by the costings of the accountants was in the case of the Darlington–Richmond branch, said to be losing £15,500 annually. It transpired, however, that they had somehow 'overlooked' the income from the War Department traffic to and from Catterick Camp, which amounted to £96,000 in 1963!

One more instance in this connection, even more recently, was a proposal to withdraw the last remaining vestige of passenger service over the important Oxford–Cambridge line, between Bletchley and Bedford. A passenger census was taken, one can only assume deliberately, when local school children, who are an important contribution to the traffic, and also many regular commuters, were on holiday! What it all boils down to is, that in simple terms, accountancy figures can be made to produce any desired result. The railways' desire to commit hari-kari in respect of many of these services, instead of making a vigorous attempt to maintain them as an essential part of the system as a whole, seems an odd way of running a business. This applies to the more widely used services, which on the face of it must be making their contribution to the revenue of the system at large. The obsolete rural branch line, with perhaps half a dozen passengers per train, four of whom would be railway servants on duty, obviously had no place in the world of today, but most of these had already disappeared by this time.

Another instance of Dr Beeching's lack of appreciation of the special requirements of a transport system was his ideal that all rolling stock, whether it be coaches, wagons, or locomotives, must be in constant use, and not allowed to lie idle. This is of course impossible in such an industry as transport, with its very wide variations in traffic density from day to day, and seasonal peaks. This point is constantly being reiterated in connection with suburban commuter traffic around London and other large centres, when the busiest service must inevitably be concentrated at two periods, but it quite ignores the obviously simple fact that if the coaches

*The Great Isle of Wight Train Robbery, published by the Railway Invigoration Society.

are not being used intensively they are also not undergoing any wear and tear while they are lying idle. They should thus last correspondingly longer, and therefore be subject to less costs in depreciation value. Dr Beeching took a particularly poor view of the large number of older passenger vehicles which were stored for many months of the year, and only put into service during the summer months, in extreme cases only being used on a few Saturdays during the height of the season. These were largely wooden vehicles of pregrouping origin, and could not have had much scrap value. If the cost of upkeep perhaps exceeded the extra revenue they earned when they were wanted, it could be justified by the fact that they enabled the railways to provide the additional services when they were most needed, and so retain the goodwill of their customers. Had they not had to turn away lucrative business, it would have helped to retain the image of the railways in the minds of the travelling public.

Apart from almost eliminating this provision of trains for the holiday season, the process was further carried to absurd lengths. The stock of reserve carriages sometimes required for normal use fell to such a low ebb that at certain large and important centres there was often simply none available, either to run a relief train when it was needed or even to strengthen a train by one or two additional coaches in a sudden upsurge of traffic due to unusual circumstances. Goods wagons again were reduced in such numbers with a sad lack of foresight during periods of slump, particularly in the coal trade, that when some recovery took place there was simply not enough available to enable requirements to be met, or to accept all of the much needed extra traffic. It is not very clear why this conception of constant use should be confined only to railways. What about motor coaches, where one reads of a busy Saturday in the summer when so many thousands of extra vehicles are reported as leaving for holiday resorts? What are these doing for the rest of the year? And where do they come from? Obviously they have not been in continual use, as Dr Beeching would like to see.

As time went on it became increasingly obvious that if the railways were really determined to close a line they would eventually do so. A pattern began to be evolved which became depressingly familiar. In an attempt to economise in rolling stock and staff, the service became awkwardly timed and generally unattractive, probably as a result of telescoping two trains into one. Passengers were discouraged

35

and driven away to other forms of transport, and then the railways would come up with sets of figures to show how much they were losing, and how necessary it was to close the line. A good example of this was the old Great Central main line to London. First, fast trains and restaurant cars disappeared, and the service was finally whittled down to three stopping trains in each direction, largely at inconvenient times. In this particular case, freight and some other non-passenger services were withdrawn first, and the remaining inadequate passenger revenue made closing inevitable. There must by now be a considerable proportion of the travelling public, apart from those who daily commute into London and other large cities, who would never dream of using the railway under any circumstances. It is a sad thought that so many of the younger generation quite frankly admit that they have never been in a train.

When Dr Beeching made the rather curious decision to change the title of British Railways to British Rail, was this a gloomy forecast of the day when there might possibly be only one main line surviving in the country, from London to Glasgow, presumably with branches to Birmingham, Liverpool and Manchester? The change was advised to senior officers purely as a publicity move, abbreviating to 'Rail' being 'snappy' and thus in fashion. It was only to be used on material seen by the public. British Railways continued to be used on all staff material, and still seems to be. There may be minor exceptions here and there.

Not all of the Beeching closure proposals have actually been implemented, at least at the time of writing, notably the suggested closure of certain lines in Wales, and of the Midland main line between Settle and Carlisle, although there is little doubt that this will succumb on completion of the West Coast electrification when the country will lose one of its most spectacular routes. The present day railway map is now in some areas, particularly the first hundred miles or so out of London north of the Thames, too much like a spider's web, shorn of the cross strands which bind it together. Cross-country communication between any of the main routes is almost non-existent. The only practical route, for instance, between Oxford and Cambridge is a lengthy and expensive detour via London. It is a fact that after leaving the outskirts of London it is possible, as an interesting and very pleasant exercise if not a route to be recommended for speed, to journey by car to near Birmingham without crossing

any railway with a passenger service. This is by keeping to side roads within the confines of the former GWR route via Banbury and the LMS via Coventry.

Among many other sundry changes of recent years which one regrets, and which seem to have stemmed from the Beeching period, may be mentioned the decision to publish only one issue of the timetables per year. This runs from each May, just prior to the introduction of what used to be the summer service, now much depleted and confined except on Saturdays only, for a limited period during the height of the season. This was of course old practice, but for the reasons already mentioned it is now but a shadow of its former self. Periodic adjustments to timings, not to mention complete alterations or withdrawals of services, are however inevitable during a period of twelve months. The result is that even before a new timetable becomes operative it is often already necessarily out of date in some respects, and has to be consulted in conjunction with an ever growing supplementary table of amendments. Gone now, too, are the comprehensive timesheets formerly found at stations. Possibly most casual passengers could not be bothered to try to understand them, and prefer to have their destinations spelled out to them in simple terms of bare train times without regard to what kind of a train they will be travelling in, where it comes from, or any other information desired by the discerning and regular traveller.

Greatest loss of all, however, is the almost complete disappearance of the conspicuous roof destination board, all trains now looking alike in their uniform anonimity. Even such famous names as the *Royal Scot, Flying Scotsman, Irish Mail, Cornish Riviera* and a host of others, now receive no more than a somewhat inconspicuous and seemingly apologetic mention in the public timetable, and one would not be surprised to see them eventually disappear entirely. I said 'almost complete' because at the time of writing, July 1971, I was delighted to see one surviving train still carrying these roof boards. Possibly the only one left, this was the daily through service which was once the 'Pines Express', still bearing the legend 'Poole–Bournemouth–Birmingham–York'.

The main result of Dr Beeching's administration of the railways during his term of office is a depressing picture of contraction on all sides. The word 'expansion' hardly enters into it at all, except perhaps in his conception of the Liner Train, for which he must be given full credit. This was in effect a development of the container principle of conveying bulk goods which could be accommodated in a separate closed van, suitable for bodily transfer to a wagon or a road vehicle and cutting out the laborious and time-consuming process of manhandling the actual goods conveyed. Dr Beeching now suggested applying the principle to through non-stop running of bulk trains, between suitable railheads where there was a large flow of traffic, in place of the slow process of individual wagons by conventional goods trains, reformed at various marshalling yards en route. Thus the Liner Train, as it was called, became a train of permanently coupled large bogie flat wagons, fully braked of course, on which large containers could be loaded for rapid conveyance at an average speed of 50mph, with the additional advantage of reliability in all weathers, and freedom from damage or pilfering. A full train totals a gross load of 680 tons with a payload of 360 tons. Dr Beeching should also be credited with the introduction of the 'merry go round' bulk coal trains between collieries and power stations, though the idea of a set of wagons shuttling to and fro between two points goes back to the 1840s when beer was conveyed in this way between Burton and Camden.

After some initial difficulties had been ironed out, such as labour disputes of the 'who does what' nature between road and rail men at the terminals, the Liner Train service was inaugurated between London and Manchester in February 1966 and eventually became well established between similar important centres. But it is unfortunate that its inherent advantages have not so far resulted in it being made use of to the extent to which it should.

Another development of a similar nature is the conveyance of new cars from manufacturer to distribution points on specially constructed trains of two-tier vehicles conveying anything up to one hundred and fifty vehicles. Here again the service is not used to the extent to which it could and should be employed, and one continues to see many of our main roads, apart from motorways, continually being cluttered up by huge juggernauts of car conveyors, quite unsuitable and unnecessary for traffic which should obviously be on the railways. It is a great pity that Dr Beeching was never given the opportunity—as was at one time suggested—of following up his railway survey by a similar investigation into the real overall cost of road transport. It would probably have proved startling to a degree.

Rail Tours

THE FIRST rail tour of the sort which became so widespread during the 1950s and 1960s was organised by the London & North Eastern Railway. In 1938 it brought out its preserved Stirling single-wheeler No 1 from York Museum, found it to be quite steamable and in good working condition, provided it with a rake of GNR six-wheeled coaches, suitably restored and repaired, and ran several trips from Kings Cross, mostly to Cambridge and back. The Railway Correspondence and Travel Society seized the opportunity and chartered its own private special to Peterborough and back on 11 September 1938. This was the first privately sponsored trip of its kind, and the war intervened before anything like it could be again attempted. This time it was the Stephenson Locomotive Society, the other of the two principal bodies engaged in outdoor railway activities at that period, which ran a modest tour

over some unusual routes in the Southern suburban area on 15 April 1950. This was the first occasion on which a special train was deliberately routed over a line not normally used for passenger trains, with the sole object of travelling over it and being in a position to mark one's map of railways traversed accordingly. In this case the highlight of the tour was the Beckenham–Norwood Junction loop, very rarely used and which had only had a brief passenger service prior to World War I. The RCTS soon followed, and the idea quickly caught on, with the result that the rest of the 1950s saw an upsurge of trips of this sort, many of them organised by other newer railway societies which sprang up during that time.

Probably the best period of all for rail tours was the earlier 1960s, when many organisations ran or attempted to run more and more trips over unusual lines, usually headed by older and disappearing classes of locomotives. It must be admitted that many of these were ill-conceived and impracticable and had to be turned down by the authorities. Others failed to get sufficient support and had to be cancelled owing to there being too many of them, often clashing with one another on dates. I was at that time actively involved as a member of the joint committee of the Railway Correspondence and Travel Society and the Stephenson Locomotive Society in arranging a number of such successful trips. I found the railways to be most co-operative at this period. Most of the regions did all they could to satisfy what were sometimes somewhat awkward and unusual requirements.

This particularly applied to the Scottish Region, especially with regard to two mammoth seven-day tours in 1960 and 1962, when we were able to cover many branch lines in Scotland which had not seen a passenger train for years and use a wide variety of steam motive power. These involved the four pre-grouping engines which had with commendable enterprise been restored specifically for working enthusiast specials, and were used as such until finding their final resting place in Glasgow Museum in June 1966. I certainly had no idea what was afoot when I visited St Rollox works in 1957 and found the Caledonian single No 123, which together with the Highland 4-6-0 No 103 had been restored for preservation before the war, stripped down in the erecting shops like any other engine for a general repair. No one seemed to know why. This idea had already been anticipated by the Great Western, which brought *City of Truro* out from York Museum and put it into working order for handling specials and even ordinary passenger services. The North Eastern Region was likewise most co-operative with regard to specialised rail tours. It would be invidious to draw comparisons between the other four except to say that the Southern was in the last year of steam more ready to accept steam haulage than the other regions. In fact many rail tours of 1967 had perforce to start from Waterloo although destined for the north, which they could do by traversing the North & South Western Junction line to Neasden Junction and thence on to the Great Central.

The Southern was also very helpful with regard to a particular brain child of my own. When I first put my idea before my committee in 1962 for bringing one of the Beattie 2-4-0Ts, then almost at the end of their life, back to London, where they had

not been seen for half a century, the immediate query was—could such a small locomotive handle a sufficiently heavy train? (Six coaches including buffet car, weighing 210 tons, was the minimum to make it economically possible.) Then why not *two* Beattie tanks? Waterloo was quite ready to consider the idea, and so it came about that a tour over some of the LSWR suburban lines took place on 2 December 1962. It was so oversubscribed that it was repeated two weeks later. One minor disability was that no steam heating could be provided owing to the lack of such apparatus on the engines, but the enormous enthusiasm seemed to make up for the lack of this particular bodily comfort. One moment of anxiety three days before the first tour occurred when Waterloo rang up to say that one of the engines had run hot at Basingstoke during its long journey from the West Country, and might have to be replaced by a M7 0-4-4T. On my stressing the point that it would rather take the edge off the uniqueness of the event, they promised to do all they could and both engines duly made their appearance. This small example is a mere indication of the many minor troubles and difficulties which often arose on these enterprises.

We were also successful in organising in conjunction with the Irish Railway Record Society and the Irish Preservation Society two never-to-be-forgotten seven day tours, entirely steam hauled, covering a good proportion of the railway system of that country in 1961 and 1964, the latter some sixteen months after the cessation of steam on CIE, thus involving special coal and watering arrangements. The pattern of rail tours changed somewhat in these later years when it was not so much a question of unusual lines and branches—the supply of which was greatly diminished anyway—as of enjoying a main line steam run purely for its own sake. With the approach of the demise of steam, British Railways itself entered the field and ran its own trips, culminating with the well known finale hauled by *Oliver Cromwell*.

It is unfortunate that up to the time of writing there has since been a complete prohibition on the use of steam trains for special occasions over BR lines in spite of the undoubted profit potential. There are at least a dozen main line express engines in private hands in tip-top working order, which could be so used. Operating difficulties and the problems of water and coal supplies are by no means unsurmountable, given the genuine attitude of co-operation. Other countries, even the USA whose rapid turn-over to diesel propulsion was on about the same scale as ours, still run their 'rail fan trips' on some railways, and they are also increasingly being accepted in other countries such as Australia and in many parts of Europe where steam is on the way out. How extraordinary then that Britain, which saw the birth of the steam locomotive and of railways in general leading directly to the industrial revolution of the 19th century, should have been so backward in honouring its epoch-making inventions, either by the issue of commemorative postage stamps, which has been done by practically every country in the world, or in perpetuating the memory of a steam locomotive in action on a grand scale.

Not all of these tours ran as smoothly as the planners hoped. Many difficulties were likely to and did occur from time to time, late running and getting out of course from the planned schedule being one of the main difficulties, apart from the occasional inevitable breakdown which was always a likelihood when elderly locomotives of a disappearing type had been specially requested. Certainly not coming under the heading of a breakdown, however, I feel I must recount a speed record which I encountered. Such distinguished authors as Mr C. J. Allen and Mr O. S. Nock have on many occasions entertained us with their experiences of some amazing feats in this direction which they have encountered in the past, so I would like to place on record my own particular favourite. The log is very simple, it was just that we managed to cover one and a half miles

in forty-four *minutes* without actually coming to a stand! It happened when returning from a tour based on Darlington, and travelling from Leeds to Manchester one Sunday evening in September 1956 by ordinary public train behind Britannia No 70033 *Charles Dickens*. The driver slowed down to walking pace outside Farnley Junction shed to set down a fireman, presumably to save him an otherwise awkward journey. Unfortunately he now faced a mile of 1 in 100 gradient, steepening to 1 in 52, before easing slightly after the first mile to 1 in 70 through Gildersome. That the driver managed to surmount this in the circumstances was I feel a remarkable feat of driving. It was difficult to see exactly what was going on in the dark, it was also wet, and there was at least one stage when we were actually slipping backwards. How many theoretical miles we must have covered by the revolution of the driving wheels it is difficult to imagine. Nevertheless, the driver managed to get the train on the move again in the right direction. A lesser man would have called for banking assistance, probably not readily available at this time on a Sunday evening, and this might have led to unwelcome enquiries as to how the situation had arisen in the first place. Needless to say we were very late at Manchester and missed our connection to Crewe and London, resulting in an all-night journey, but this was just one of the hazards one had to risk on these exciting and never-to-be-forgotten occasions.

Preservation

PRESERVATION OF all sorts of railway equipment and rolling stock, with locomotives at the head of the list, is no new thing, and fortunately many examples have survived from the nineteenth century in various museums, even if there are some regrettable gaps in continuity. The modern preservation movement of something more than a mere static exhibit, however, was started in 1950 by the threatened closure of the small narrow-gauge Talyllyn Railway in Wales. This had only managed to keep going by virtue of its owner, Sir Haydn Jones, who had subsidised it in its later years from his own resources. On his death its end seemed inevitable, but a band of enthusiasts from the Birmingham area investigated the possibility of maintaining it in run-

ning order as a working museum piece. It would be supported by subscriptions from interested persons and, even more important, by voluntary labour. So was born the Talyllyn Railway Preservation Society, its initial troubles and ultimate success being too well known to be recapitulated here. It was soon followed by the neighbouring Festiniog, a more difficult proposition as this line had lain derelict for several years and needed complete resuscitation, whereas the Talyllyn in its own words 'never closed'.

Since those pioneer days, a large number of similar projects have come into being, not only in this country but all over the world. Not all achieved fruition, but many did, and we now have a number of other societies which have succeeded in opening or reopening various branch lines, or portions thereof, both narrow and standard gauge. These run a service of trains, usually confined to weekends during the summer months, and needless to say steam hauled. The Keighley & Worth Valley, however, does run an all the year round Saturdays only service, usually worked by a diesel railbus, for the benefit of the local inhabitants wishing to travel to Keighley for their shopping. All of these railways are manned by voluntary labour; it is only this that makes them a practicable proposition, but the supply of enthusiasts willing and able to devote such a lot of their spare time and energies is limited. Other less ambitious projects are the various groups that have acquired a few locomotives together with a yard and perhaps a few hundred yards length of line over which they can be steamed. One very important venture was the establishment of the Standard Gauge Steam Trust, which acquired part of the former GWR shed and workshops at Tyseley, Birmingham, with full facilities for major repairs of locomotives. The many restored to working order in private hands all over the country will eventually require such attention in the course of time, particularly if and when they are once more permitted to run excursions over British Rail main lines. There are now several hundred locomotives of all types, from main line express engines to humble industrials, preserved all over the country, mainly by private individuals and groups. For particulars of these one must be referred to the various books which have been published on the subject, in particular the author's own book—'Preserved Locomotives', which gives full detailed histories and illustrations.

It is only possible here to refer briefly to the several museums at which locomotives are to be found on static display, such as the Science Museum, Kensington, where may be seen among other exhibits, the original *Rocket* of G. Stephenson. Then there is the splendid collection got together by the LNER at York, the only pre-nationalisation railway to embark on such a project, during the 1920s. Some of these, including *Columbine* and *Gladstone*, were evacuated during the war to the lonely NBR shed at Reedsmouth, in Northumberland, for safe keeping. More recent projects include a few reasonably representative GWR types to be found in the Swindon Corporation Museum, among them *City of Truro*. Many other local authorities have locomotives on display, as instanced by the Glasgow Corporation Transport Museum, while there are more at Belfast, Leicester, and other large cities, and the National Trust Industrial Railway Museum at Penrhyn Castle, Bangor, North Wales.

Lastly, there is the splendid collection at Clapham, opened by BR in conjunction with London Transport on 29 March 1961. Here, at the time of writing, is to be found not only the finest display under one roof in the world of locomotives, carriages, and all manner of railway equipment and relics, but in addition several tramcars, omnibuses and so on, the property of London Transport. British Railways have also a number of other locomotives which were put aside on withdrawal. So far it has not been able to accommodate these for display, and they have had to be stored away from public view until room can be found.

It was in 1958 that, at the request of the chairman of the Transport Commission, a consultative panel of experts was set up to consider carefully what railway relics of all sorts should be set aside for preservation as and when they became available. Some fifty locomotives of many varieties and classes were selected, this being inclusive of those already to be found at York, and a number of others temporarily stored at Crewe, Derby, Horwich and Glasgow. Eventually this somewhat formidable list had to be whittled down to some extent owing to the difficulties of housing all of them safely in vandal-proof situations, but room was found at Clapham for over a dozen of them. A few others have been handed over to some reputable organisations on a permanent loan basis.

Unfortunately Clapham itself, after having been opened for only three years, came under fire from high quarters in BR—it will be seen that this was soon after Dr Beeching had arrived on the scene. BR was becoming restless at the alleged loss incurred in its upkeep; it also claimed that the site was too valuable to remain indefinitely as a museum and that the collection should be moved elsewhere. It was further suggested that a national collection of this sort should no longer be the responsibility of BR, and that it should be taken over by the Ministry of Education, which already administered the Science and the Victoria and Albert Museums. Approaches were accordingly made on these lines to the government of the day, but to no avail. St Pancras was put forward as a possible alternative at a time when there seemed a likelihood of it no longer being used as a passenger station, but it was found that it could not be dispensed with after all. It was then proposed that the old engine roundhouses at York should be converted to a museum and the Clapham exhibits moved there. There were very many objections to this, and not only those of having the country's major transport museum located away from London. There were doubts as to whether the space would accommodate all of the BR exhibits from Clapham (quite apart from the London Transport collection, which would have to be found a new home), to say nothing of the other engines awaiting eventual display or any new desirable additions, electric and diesel, essential to maintain a continuing story of railway development in general.

Early in 1971, another idea was being actively pursued by the consultative panel already referred to (to which Mr J. H. Scholes, museum curator of BR, has been acting in consultation ever since its inception), together with Lord Eccles, Minister for Education and Science. Attention had been directed to the possibility of converting part of the station at Crystal Palace, possibly with an upper tier to accommodate the London Transport exhibits also. It would have had the great advantage of having direct rail connection; the lack of this at Clapham and its considerable distance from any suitable transfer point for the conveyance of engines and other large exhibits was a severe handicap.

Most regrettably, in May 1971, the Government turned down this idea on the grounds of expense, notwithstanding that the estimated cost of around a million pounds would have been chicken feed compared with the vast expenditure being incurred in other directions. It now seems inevitable that the fine collection at Clapham will be dispersed, many of the railway exhibits going to York, although there will not be room for them all, let alone any new additions, while the fate of the magnificent collection of trams and London Transport exhibits has not yet been resolved. Some small consolation may lie in the fact that at York the engines will be with ready rail access. No major road transfer operation will be involved when the day again comes, as we all hope it will, when perhaps the stirring sight of *Mallard* or the Midland compound shall once more be proudly seen on one of our main lines, just as GNR No 1 was in 1938. It could and should be done!

Since the above was written, and at the last minute before going to press, it was announced that, as an experiment, GWR *King George V* was to be allowed to make a tour comprising visits to Birmingham and London, the first steam train to traverse a main line in this country for over three years. It is to be hoped that by the time this book appears further such ventures will have become an established fact.

The Present and the Future

OF RECENT years one of the most noticeable developments has been in the matter of increased train speeds made possible by electrification and diesel working, speeds which would have been quite impracticable day in and day out under ordinary conditions with steam propulsion, even if something approaching them could have been, and in many cases was, achieved with steam on special occasions on very limited selected services. One has only to look at the present day schedules on such 'Inter City' trains, as they are now known, as those between Euston and Liverpool, Paddington and Bristol, or Kings Cross and Newcastle, although the latter is not such a very great improvement on the pre-war timing of the *Silver Jubilee*. The emphasis on present day services is once more on faster trains between the principal cities and towns with regular-interval timings, a timetable system inaugurated many years ago by the Southern Railway on its electrified suburban services, but not much practised until recently on longer distance main line timetables. The old Midland Railway was probably the innovator, for in pre-grouping days this enterprising line made some play of its regular departures from St Pancras for Manchester at twenty-five minutes past the hour every two hours continuously from 4.25 am to 6.25 pm. Now, very many years later, the general pattern is repeated in the standard departure time of .05 past every hour of main line expresses to the north.

Signalling developments, too, have been proceeding apace with more colour lights, track circuiting, increased automatic train control from a few centrally situated signal boxes, and the gradual disappearance of the wayside signal cabin and semaphore signal. Closely allied to this is the wholesale removal of running loops, refuge sidings, and crossovers, consequent on the higher general speed of freight trains and the decline in freight traffic in general. The natural result of higher average speeds is of course the shorter occupation time of the sections. Some four track main line has been reduced to two in places, and even formerly busy double track routes have been singled. This economises on maintenance costs, but has very regrettable results in timekeeping, when an engine failure occurs on a single line stretch, with somewhat disastrous consequences to the crossing arrangements of trains travelling in the opposite direction. A very typical example of this is the case of most of the former Southern Railway route between Salisbury and Exeter, now operated by the Western region. Once a busy main line, it is now regarded as of very secondary importance, although the maximum speed limit is still no less than eighty miles per hour, much higher than on any other single line section.

It is accepted that freight trains can be speeded up by concentrating traffic at a number of centres for distribution by road by National Carriers Limited, a wholly owned subsidiary. But it is difficult to accept the desirability or economics of the complete closure of so many goods yards on lines still open. Much important wagon load traffic has deliberately been thrown away to the roads. Wagon loads of coal could be left for local coal merchants to unload themselves at very little expense to the railways. This helped in the relief of road congestion, avoiding the necessity of large lorries from the nearest (although often not at all near) concentration depot cluttering up the roads.

The running of British Railways since nationalisation has not been easy, quite apart from the inevitable gradual decline in the face of increasing road competition. The four changes of government, respectively labour, conservative, labour and again conservative, did not exactly help, for the railways became a political football kicked around by successive parties with a somewhat divergent view on the importance of railways. Whatever one's political views as a whole, it cannot be denied that the socialist party has, generally speaking, been more favourably disposed to the railways than the conservatives. This was particularly evident during the labour regime of 1964–70, when Mrs Barbara Castle, as Minister of Transport, tried to call a halt to any further rail closures under the Beeching plan. Those already implemented were regarded as having exceeded the limits to which the plan should be pursued, with due regard to the economy of the country and the social necessity of adequate rail communication. That government recognised the need to retain as far as possible what was left of the truncated railway system. Indeed by introducing what has become known as 'grant aid', it agreed to furnish an annual subsidy for a limited number of years in respect of lines or services essential to the community which were reported to be running at a loss. At the time of writing there are indications that the present conservative government will not be prepared to extend this indefinitely. It has already imposed severe limitations for the future, with hints that the railways should once more attempt to pay their way, reverting to an impossible ideal already found in all countries to be impracticable under modern conditions. This problem is beginning to manifest itself not only as regards railways, but is being increasingly felt by public road transport as well.

The turnover of staff at the top level has also been far too great, even where politics were not involved. There were too many appointments to high office of non-railwaymen, who whatever qualifications they may have had for the direction of a large industry, could not have the necessary experience so essential to appreciate the particular problems of railway operation. One classic case of stupidity or short-sightedness was that of Gerard Fiennes, old-time railwayman, who as general manager of the Eastern Region was summarily sacked by Sir Stanley Raymond for attempting to run a railway as it should be run. Raymond himself was relieved of his job by Barbara Castle shortly afterwards. For the last few years there has at least been a genuine railwayman at the top, Sir Henry Johnson, but unfortunately due for retirement in 1971. He has been replaced by Mr Richard Marsh, who was for a time Minister of Transport in the last labour government. At the time of writing he has only just assumed his new post and it is not yet possible to predict what effect this will have on the future policies and fortunes of the railway system.

Before the war and immediately afterwards, the main threat to the railways was felt from the omnibus and the long distance coach, but it is now the private car and growth of transport by heavy goods lorries made easier by the construction of motorways. Much of this traffic is far more suitable for conveyance by rail, and means should have been found to restrict it to such. Even the aeroplane has become a competitor to be reckoned with, but its opportunities are limited in such a small island as ours. To the private car there is of course no answer, and this must be accepted as a natural and inevitable phase of a changing world. Even the omnibus, once the railways' principal rival, is now itself unable to cope with the competition, and many rural bus services which were put on to replace closed railway branches are now in turn facing the threat of withdrawal. Those put on in place of the former M & GNJR, for instance, have already almost entirely disappeared. There are some who maintain that on a long term basis there may be no place for railways in this country. I hope and believe this not to be the case, for rail travel under its most favourable conditions still remains not only the most pleasant, comfortable, relaxing and reliable (trains can run when weather conditions bring all other forms of transport to a standstill) form of travel, but above all the safest. This is still the author's considered opinion, despite his near approach to liquidation already referred to.

At the time of writing it is announced that after proposals, counter-suggestions, objections and experiments lasting over a hundred years, the Channel Tunnel may now become an accomplished fact. Both Governments concerned, British and French, have agreed that it can go ahead with the proviso that so far as this country is concerned it must be financed under private enterprise. In the 1860s it would have been a hazardous operation with no previous experience of the difficulties bound to occur—even a project such as the Severn Tunnel was at that time a dream of the future—but the technical difficulties should today present no undue problems. Although most of the traffic would consist of the conveyance of road vehicles, the possibilities of running through trains, passenger or freight, between England and the Continent might well give a fillip to rail transport as a whole. One can only hope so.

What then of the future? At the time of writing, summer 1971, there is already under construction at Derby a new train designed for speeds of up to 155 mph, with average speeds between cities of well over 100 mph, intended to give definite and worthwhile advantage over the private car for distances of more than seventy miles or so. It will increase the distance from London or any other centre from which it will be possible to conduct a day's business or shopping. It will, for instance, be much more practicable to travel from London to Newcastle and back for the day than at present. Known as the Advanced Passenger Train, each unit will consist of four coaches, aero-dynamically streamlined with bullet nosed power cars, each fitted with four 300hp gas turbine engines. Experience of the London-Manchester and Liverpool electrification has shown that a large proportion of the passenger journeys were newly generated rather than captured from other modes of travel, although a not inconsiderable part was diverted from air. The rise in average speed thus increased the distance over which rail travel can successfully compete with air travel, quite apart from the added advantage of general comfort and amenities. It is anticipated that these new trains might well be able to reduce the present six-hour journey between London and Glasgow to four hours.

Looking beyond the more immediate future, with the phenomenal scientific and technical advances now occurring in all walks of life at an ever increasing rate in the name of 'progress', it is quite impossible to forecast what form of transport we shall be using in fifty years' time. However, with the utmost imagination one cannot visualise the mass movement of hundreds of thousands of workers in such a dense area as London other than by some form of rail transport. Its ability to contain a maximum number of persons, even without undue overcrowding, in a minimum of space, no doubt in the future in automatic driverless trains, can surely not conceivably be matched by any other form of transport. Time alone can show.

A Brief Diary of some Interesting Dates and Events

1939

28 May : Tolworth – Chessington line completed by SR. The last standard gauge completely new passenger railway to be built in the country, apart from London Underground extensions, new loops, connecting lines and so on

15 Aug : Emergency Powers Defence Act empowered Ministry of Transport to take over railways

1 Sept-4 Sep : Mass evacuation of children from London and other large centres to country areas

3 Sep : Declaration of war by England and France against Germany

11 Sep : Drastic cuts in train services. Restaurant cars and most sleeping cars withdrawn. All privately owned wagons requisitioned, except those designed for special traffic

24 Sept : Special excursion trains and bookings withdrawn

25 Sep : First emergency timetable published by GWR, followed by other railways

8 Oct : Metropolitan Railway Pullman cars withdrawn

9 Oct : Cheap day tickets withdrawn

16 Oct : Some restaurant cars reinstated

December : MOT placed orders for 240 2-8-0s of LMS class 8F design. Work suspended on electrification of Manchester – Sheffield – Wath line

1940

May : Collapse of France

27 May-4 Jun: Dunkirk evacuation. Operation 'Dynamo'. 319,000 troops saved and conveyed in 620 trains from Channel ports, principally Dover

1 Jul : Channel Islands occupied by Germany

1941

9 May : Ministry of War Transport formed

16 May : Lord Stamp, chairman of LMS, killed in air raid

1942

5 Oct : Cheap day fares and restaurant cars finally withdrawn for duration of war. Unnecessary travel discouraged

11 Dec : First of a large number of USA built 2-8-0s to arrive in this country exhibited at a short ceremony at Paddington

1943

February: Appearance of first War Dept 2-8-0s, designed by R. A. Riddles. Total of 935 eventually completed

1944

22 Feb : Outline of plans for invasion of France, operation 'Overlord', secretly conveyed to selected railwaymen of various grades by General (later Field Marshal) Montgomery

1 Apr : Closure of Wick and Lybster branch, Britain's most remote line from London

6 Jun : D-Day. Invasion of France

1945

8 May : VE day (Victory in Europe)

26 Jul : Socialist government elected

15 Aug : VJ day (Victory over Japan)

30 Sep : Bourne End accident

1 Oct : Restoration of some restaurant cars by LMS, LNER and SR. Lineside apparatus for picking up and setting down mailbags from TPO's brought into use again (had been suspended at outbreak of war). Restoration of GNR suburban service to Aldersgate, and through to Moorgate on 6 May 1946

23 Oct : Continental boat trains resumed between Victoria and Dover

19 Nov : Sir Herbert Morrison announced Labour government's plans for nationalisation of railways

31 Dec : Restaurant cars restored on GWR

1946

1 Apr : Ministry of War Transport abolished

15 Apr : 'Golden Arrow' service resumed (worked on first day by the first of Bulleid's wartime pacifics No 21C1 *Channel Packet*). GWR Weymouth – Channel Islands service resumed

During year : Complete renumbering of LNER on a logical classification basis in place of numbers inherited from the pre-grouping companies

1947

6 Aug : Passing of Transport Bill for nationalisation of railways

31 Oct : Plans announced for electrification to Ramsgate and Dover, also to Hastings via Tonbridge and the Oxted line, but these two were not carried out

December : Appearance of LMS No 10000, Britain's first main line diesel electric locomotive

1948

1 Jan : Railways passed from government control, to newly formed British Transport Commission, embracing the four main line companies and a number of small ones

30 Jan : Display at Addison Road for official inspection of four engines painted in alternative proposed new liveries for British Railways

10 Aug : Former LMS lines in Northern Ireland transferred to Ulster Transport Authority

12 Aug : Centenary of death of George Stephenson

19 Oct : Opening of Rugby Testing Plant (promoted jointly by LMS and LNER prior to outbreak of war). Appropriately No 60007 *Sir Nigel Gresley* was the first engine to be tested

1949

1 Feb : Report of London Plan Committee suggesting rail improvements in London area

26 Sep : Commencement of electrification between Liverpool Street and Shenfield

1950
2 Apr : First of several regional boundary adjustments

1951
Report on future electrification policy, amplifying the Weir report of 1931, recommending 1500 volts DC overhead, apart from the Southern region. Socialist government replaced by Conservative

31 Dec : British Transport Commission discontinued financing the former LNWR owned Dundalk Newry & Greenore Railway in Ireland

1952
15 Feb : Funeral train of King George VI, hauled by No 4082 *Windsor Castle* from Paddington to Windsor

8 Oct : Harrow accident, the second most disastrous in the history of railways in the British Isles

1953
6 May : Transport Bill under which the Railway Executive would be abolished as from 30 Sep, with decentralisation of regions, each with its own manager

1954
14 Sep : Commencement of electrified passenger service between Manchester and Sheffield. Britain's first full scale main line electrification

1955
25 Jan : Sir Brian Robertson announced plans for modernisation, including the eventual replacement of steam by diesel and electrification

27 Mar : Reconstructed station at Potters Bar brought into use, first stage of widening this section of the old GNR main line to four tracks

28 May-14 Jun : Strike by ASLEF. NUR not involved and some services maintained

15 Jun : Introduction of car sleeper trains between Kings Cross and Perth

1956
3 June : 3rd class accommodation redesignated 2nd class

October : Last engine of pre-nationalisation design to be built. GWR type pannier tank No 3409

31 Dec : Closure of Liverpool Overhead Railway, Britain's only city elevated line and one of the few still independent systems left outside nationalisation

1957
3 Jun : Delivery from English Electric of first of planned types of diesel electric locos, BO-BO No D8000

4 Dec : Lewisham accident

1958
1 Jan : Pre-grouping titles 'Great Northern' and 'Great Eastern' areas officially revived by Eastern region

24 Jul : Inspection by Sir Brian Robertson at Marylebone of first Derby built diesel electric loco under modernisation plan, BO-BO No D5000

1959
28 Feb : Closure of a large portion of the Midland & Great Northern Joint Railway, the first lengthy main line to be abandoned

16 Mar : First electric trains on Clacton and Walton branches

4 Apr : Opening of new tunnel bores between Hadley Wood and Potters Bar

3 May : Completion of Hadley Wood - Potters Bar widening

2 Jun : First through electric train between Victoria and Ramsgate hauled by electric locos E5003 and E5004

3 Jun : First multiple unit trains to Ramsgate

1960
5 Jan : Closure of Swansea & Mumbles Tramway, the world's oldest public railway

18 Mar : Ceremony at Swindon, naming of last steam loco to be built by BR No 92220 *Evening Star*, by Mr K. W. C. Grand, general manager of WR, presided over by R. F. Hanks, chairman of Western area board

9 Sep : Last slip carriage, at Bicester North, off 5.10 pm train Paddington to Wolverhampton

12 Sep : First stage of LM electrification inaugurated between Manchester and Crewe

20 Sep : Last steam suburban train left Liverpool Street, 9.25 pm to Hertford East, hauled by N7 0-6-2T No 69685. Finale to the world's most intensified steam suburban service, introduced by the GER in the early 1920s

7 Nov : Electrification of Glasgow suburban services north of the Clyde between Helensburgh Balloch and Airdrie

26 Nov : First new power signal box (panel type) on WR opened at Plymouth

1961
5 Feb : First barrier type crossing controlled automatically by track circuits. Spath, near Uttoxeter (removed 25 Jan 1965 on closure of line)

29 Mar : Opening of first part of National Transport Museum at Clapham

May : Last publication of 'Bradshaw' timetable

1 Jun : Dr R. Beeching appointed as chairman of BTC as successor to Sir Brian Robertson

6 Nov : Electric services commenced on former LT & SR Fenchurch Street - Shoeburyness

1962
January : Crewe - Liverpool electrification

27 May : Glasgow suburban electrification. 'Blue Trains' commenced running south of the Clyde

1 Aug : New Transport Act. BTC to be dissolved and functions divided between several new boards

9 Sep : Disappearance of steam in East Anglia, the first area to be completely dieselised

1963
1 Jan : Pullman Car Company merged into BR

27 Mar : Dr Beeching's report on the reshaping of BR system

8 Aug : The great train robbery near Cheddington. Up night postal halted by interference with colour light signals and several million pounds worth of used

banknotes stolen

6 Oct : First new power signal box (panel type) on LMR opened at Nuneaton

1964
14-15 Jun : 24 hour clock notation introduced by all regions for public timetables

6 July : New power signal box opened at Watford

14 Sep : New power signal box opened at Rugby

1965
30 Jan : Funeral train of Sir Winston Churchill on his last journey worked from Waterloo by pacific No 34051 bearing his name

14 Mar : Bushey and Castlethorpe water troughs taken out of use on fast lines

26 Sep : Bushey and Castlethorpe water troughs taken out of use on slow lines

4 Oct : Christleton and Prestatyn water troughs taken out of use

18 Nov : Completion of electrification into Euston, first energised on this date

1966
3 Jan : Full electric working between Euston and Crewe, and speed limit raised to maximum 90 mph (later increased to 100 mph between Willesden and Rugby)

28 Feb : Introduction of Beeching's 'freightliner' trains, initially between London and Manchester

6 Mar : Closure of Somerset & Dorset Joint line

1967
Between 2 Apr & 11 Jun : Southern Railway West of England main line singled between Wilton and Pinhoe

10 Jul : Completion of Bournemouth electrification SR

5 Nov : Hither Green accident

1968
6 Jan : Hixon level crossing accident

3 Aug : Last two ordinary scheduled trains to be worked by steam left Preston behind class 5 4-6-0s Nos 45212 to Blackpool and 45318 to Liverpool Exchange

11 Aug : Last commemorative steam tour run by British Railways, Liverpool and Manchester to Carlisle and back

Illustrations

The War Years

The companion volume *Railways Between the Wars*, to which this book is designed as a sequel, finished with a photograph taken in September 1939. This depicted the evacuation of children from London in anticipation of the expected air raids, which did not in fact materialise for several months. It is appropriate therefore that the story should be taken up at this point with a similar illustration, this time of a station in Hertfordshire, to which children had been brought from a resort on the Kent coast on 20 July 1941 when the threat of invasion was still a very serious one. This third major evacuation was not on such a large scale as those of September 1939 and June 1940, when air raids began, but 291 special trains were run.

London evacuee children at Yeovil in November 1939, waiting to meet their parents, who are visiting them on the specially organised Children's Sunday Excursion.

A London underground station given over in the early days of the war to shelter from threatened air attacks. Many others on which services were still maintained also provided similar accommodation on the platforms during the night.

Handling mail in blackout conditions at Euston. Travel posters still remain on the walls.

A typical wartime scene at Paddington in May 1942 with servicemen on leave and female ticket collectors. Women were able to undertake many duties so as to release railwaymen for more strenuous jobs or into the forces.

Bomb damage at Newton Abbot, 20 August 1940. Pannier tank No 2787 and 4–6–0 No 6811 *Cranbourne Grange*.

Another bomb 'incident' on the Great Western, near Bristol. 2–6–0 No 4358 did not get very far on this occasion when working the 7.10 pm train to Salisbury on 6 December 1940.

Damage at St Pancras, 10 May 1941, fortunately not so severe as it might have been. Barlow's mighty arched roof of 1868 withstood the effects of the Luftwaffe and the magnificent frontage, clock tower, and former hotel buildings narrowly escaped what might have been irreparable disaster.

Paddington also 'bought one' on 22 March 1944, but again without too much effect on the train shed itself.

The big freeze of January 1940 also added to the difficulties of railway operation during these early months of the war. A snowed-up train is seen here near Chinley, on the MR Derby-Manchester line.

The evacuation from Dunkirk placed an enormous burden on the Southern Railway. The operation known as 'Dynamo' involved the running of no less than 620 special trains in the period of nine days starting on 27 May 1940 for the conveyance of 319,000 troops from channel ports, principally Dover, to Redhill for dispersal to other parts of the country. It was a masterpiece of organisation, improvised at short notice. One of the problems was the supply of refreshments to the weary travellers, and the trains were halted at such wayside stations as Headcorn and Paddock Wood, where RASC troops, assisted by many local ladies, worked continuously in long daily and nightly shifts to supply this urgent need. Above is a scene at Addison Road, Kensington, on 31 May 1940, when men from the British Expeditionary Force were being served with refreshments. Not only food, but essential items of clothing such as socks were also an urgent necessity, and these are seen being distributed at Paddock Wood on 1 June 1940.

The Prime Minister, Sir Winston Churchill, at work during one of his numerous train journeys.

The kind of heavy wartime load which had to be carried by the railways in thousands of special trains during these hectic years. Guns on Admiralty Set, at Exeter St Davids, 20 June 1941.

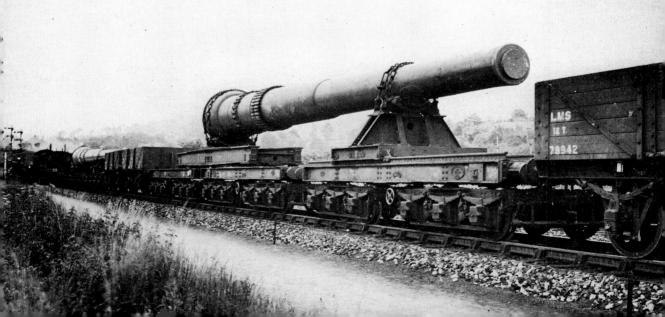

Many passenger coaches were adapted for use in hospital trains behind the fighting areas. This LMS brake third, built at Derby in 1930 as No 6196 and renumbered 5334 in 1933, was converted at Swindon to a pharmacy car as WD 5208. It was lost in France in 1940.

Among the railway owned ships also given over to wartime needs was the *Saint David*, owned by the Fishguard & Rosslare Railways & Harbour Co, a twin screw steam turbine vessel of 2702 tons constructed by Messrs Cammel Laird & Co Ltd in 1932. It took part in the Dunkirk evacuation.

Cold Meece, a new station at the end of a freshly constructed branch line, built under conditions of secrecy to serve a Royal Ordnance Corps factory at Swynnerton, Stafford-shire, a small village with a pre-war population of less than a thousand. Apart from the works depot, there was also a USAF base at Cold Meece used by thousands of Americans. The branch was one mile 1307 yards long, connecting at Swynnerton Junction with the old North Stafford railway from Stone to Norton Bridge on the LNWR main line.

The branch was double track, and the station itself consisted of four platforms hand-ling at its maximum use five trains in twenty-five minutes. At the height of the war it carried three million people a year, workmen travelling from various parts of the Pot-teries, but as it never appeared in any public timetable or railway map it was little known. Opened on 3 August 1941, it remained in operation until 27 June 1958 when the branch was entirely closed.

The USA built several hundred 2–8–0s for war use, mainly in Western Europe, but they were designed to British loading gauge so that they could be used in this country, as indeed many of them were. This view shows one of the first of them which received a brief official inspection at Paddington on 11 December 1942.

Although a lot of the USA 2–8–0s worked in this country during the war years, pictures of them are scarce owing to the restrictions and difficulties of obtaining photographs. This rare view shows Nos 2148 and 1892 between Wootton Bassett and Swindon, actual date unknown, but probably some time in 1944, as the former is known to have been working from Oxley shed in April of that year, and No 1892 was also reported from Aberdare at about that time.

For shunting duties were these 0–6–0T 'switching' engines, in USA parlance, with typical American features such as bar frames, and inevitably outside cylinders. Not many of them worked in this country, although the Southern Railway acquired fourteen of them after the war for use in Southampton Docks. One of these is still in active use on the Keighley & Worth Valley Railway, and there are also three others in the hands of preservation societies. This view shows a collection of them stored in sidings at Newbury Racecourse in March 1947 awaiting disposal. Note the various styles of lettering.
US troops entraining at Liverpool Riverside on arrival from America.

Although not a wartime design, the Stanier 8Fs, having originated on the LMS in 1935, were adopted for general construction in the first years of the war and were in fact built by all four of the pre-nationalisation companies in their own workshops. Some of them even ran as LNER engines. Many of them were sent to the Middle East. This fairly typical view of a well known class shows No 48547 crossing Denthead Viaduct, on the Midland Settle—Carlisle line, in 1951.

In 1943 there appeared the first new design of locomotive constructed for purely wartime needs. Known as the 'Austerities', these 2–8–0s were the product of Mr R. A. Riddles, then associated with the Ministry of Supply, and later to become CME on British Railways. No less than 935 were eventually built. Many were sent overseas and some never came back. After the war the LNER acquired 200 of them, and eventually 733 came into the possession of British Railways. This particular engine, seen climbing Beattock Bank in 1951, started life as WD 7165, worked for a time in Scotland, then went to the Continent; at one time it was Dutch State Railways No 4483. It returned to this country after the cessation of hostilities, worked for a while on the GWR, and finally became BR No 90152. It was scrapped in 1965. This is a typical sample of the histories of many of this interesting class.

Travel in wartime. Scene outside Paddington in 1944 with a mile long queue of holiday-makers hopefully awaiting admission to the platforms. Owing to the restrictions on extra trains, a special appeal had to be made in this case to a very high level of authority before any relaxation could be hurriedly improvised.

A quick return to comparatively comfortable travel. Scene at Kingswear, Devon, on 25 August 1945, only three months after VE Day, and just two weeks after final victory, VJ Day.

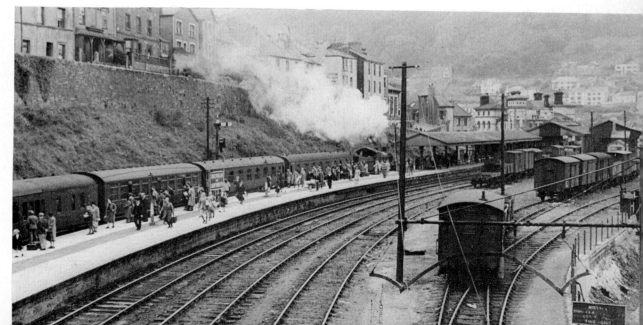

Steam since 1939

Few new locomotive designs appeared from the former main line companies during the war years, but among them were the somewhat startling Q1 0–6–0s on the Southern, designed by Mr O. V. Bulleid and following shortly after his even more unconventional 'Merchant Navy' Pacifics.

Forty of these, Nos C1-C40, were turned out from Brighton and Ashford in 1942. During the latter stages of the war they proved to be extremely useful engines, being powerful and yet having a wide route availability. No C22 seen here in Eastleigh works in 1947.

Bulleid experimental mixed traffic engine of 1949, with driving cab at either end and the boiler offset to one side amidships. With many other unusual features, teething troubles were abundant, and with Mr Bulleid's departure BR lost interest in continuing the experiments. Of three engines built, only one was ever steamed, and they quietly faded out of existence. Seen here at Eastleigh in 1950. With perseverance, they might well have taken their full share in prolonging the life of steam in this country.

The last LMS design of H. G. Ivatt, which appeared just before nationalisation. Only the first three, Nos 3000-3002, appeared in LMS livery. The next one, turned out from Horwich in January 1948, came out as BR No M3003. Their somewhat ungainly appearance was not helped by the double blast pipe chimney, but fortunately these were found to be of doubtful advantage on this particular class and they were replaced by ordinary chimneys. Seen here at Bletchley in April 1948.

The last of the many GWR 4–6–0 designs, dating back to the original Dean engine of 1902, and perpetuated by his successors, Churchward, Collett and Hawksworth, remained true to general tradition, and differed in general outline only by such details as the elongated continuous splashers. No 1019 *County of Merioneth* at Swindon in April 1946.

The post-war 'Golden Arrow' all-Pullman between Victoria and Dover, with direct connection to Paris, was reinstated on 15 April 1946. It is seen here passing Tonbridge on 26 April 1947 hauled by one of the new 'West Country' Pacifics, No 21C156, Bulleid's new method of numbering. Under BR this engine became No 34056 and was named *Croydon*.

During 1946 the LNER carried out a complete renumbering of its locomotives. Since 1923 it had perpetuated their pregrouping numbers, suitably increased by a requisite number of thousands according to their line of origin (GNR engines, for instance, added 3000). A scheme was now inaugurated under which all were renumbered together in groups according to type, classification, and so on.

As a reaction against the drabness of the wartime years, when all engines were painted unlined black, the LNER decided to revert to green for all classes, although it was implemented in very few cases so far as the smaller types were concerned before being overtaken by nationalisation. It was however very sensibly applied to the station pilots at the principal large stations, where the engines were so much in the public eye. North British 0–6–0T No 8477 (late 9830) at Edinburgh Waverley in 1947.

Immediately after nationalisation, engines were given prefixes to their existing numbers to avoid possible confusion, LMS engines receiving the letter 'M', LNER 'E', GWR 'W' and SR 'S'. It was decided however to add as a general rule 30000 to SR numbers, 40000 to LMS, and 60000 to LNER, GWR remaining unaltered, as they had cast number plates, unsuitable for alteration, whereas the other three had used painted numbers. Rebuilt 'Royal Scot' *The Boy Scout*, seen here passing Berkhamsted on 6 November 1949, was a temporary oddity in that for a time it carried both its new number and the letter 'M', in this case in the form of a suffix.

A new class of suburban tank engine had been introduced by Mr Thompson on the LNER in 1945. The first four came out as LNER 9000-9003, followed in 1948 by E9004-E9012, the temporary scheme adopted until the complete renumbering scheme was introduced, under which the next three became 69013-69015. By then it had been discovered that there was not sufficient room in the 8000-8999 block allocated to shunting engines, to accommodate new construction. The 2–6–4Ts were therefore altered to start, oddly enough, at 67701, not 67700 in accordance with the more sensible and normal pattern, and the whole class eventually ran from 67701-67800. No E9011 (shortly to become 67712) seen here leaving Shenfield with a Southend train in June 1948. It still carries green livery, together with the words 'British Railways' in full. This was initially applied by all four regions, usually in the style of lettering used by the former companies. Note the overhead wires in connection with the forthcoming electrification, also the NER clerestory van.

1951 saw the appearance of the first of the new standard designs—twelve in all —adopted for future construction. This view shows a group of them arranged for public exhibition in Willesden shed in May 1954. It consists of 2-6-4T No 80084, Britannia No 70037 *Hereward the Wake*, class 5 No 73050 and class 3 2-6-0 No 77009, while on the extreme left can be seen the front of the three-cylinder Pacific No 71000 *Duke of Gloucester*, designed for top link express work. Unfortunately it was destined to be the only one to be built, owing to the sudden decision to change over from steam to diesel propulsion.

Of all the new standard designs, the last, the class 9 2-10-0, was almost undoubtedly the best of all. Although 251 of them were built they were soon ruthlessly to be consigned to the scrap heap after only a few years of active life, an unwarrantable and inexcusable waste of much fine machinery. A variation in the design was the construction of ten engines with Italian 'Crosti' boilers, an advanced form of feed water heating by means of an additional drum below the boiler itself to conserve some of the heat normally exhausted into the atmosphere. Another somewhat halfhearted experiment was the fitting of the Giesl multiple jet exhaust ejector, designed to effect considerable economies in coal consumption, and used with satisfactory results on some European railways. It was however only tried out on two engines by British Railways, one of them being class 9 2-10-0 No 92250 (seen here at Gloucester in May 1961). A more unsuitable type could hardly have been chosen if the object had really been to give the apparatus a fair and reasonable trial, as these engines were already an extremely efficient design, and the claimed improvement only showed up to marked advantage in much older types. It can only be assumed that the choice was deliberate, as by this time BR had reached the stage when it was not only not interested, but would probably actively discourage anything which might possibly improve the efficiency of the steam locomotive.

Diesel and Electric Traction

Pre-war Southern Railway suburban unit, composed of converted pregrouping stock. Many such sets were still in service when this photograph was taken at Clapham Junction on 14 June 1957.

SR electric No 20002 (formerly CC2), the second of two built by Mr Bulleid in 1941 and 1945 respectively, a third following in 1948. This Region relies almost entirely on multiple unit traction, even for its express services. These three locomotives were chiefly used on freight work, but this one is seen leaving Brighton on 10 June 1950 with the through Birkenhead-Hastings train. A few more engines of a new design were built by BR in 1958 for working Continental boat trains.

One of seven express locomotives introduced in 1954 for working over the newly electrified LNER line between Manchester and Sheffield. Passenger services were withdrawn from this section in 1970, the trains being diverted to the former Midland route via Dore & Totley and, of course, diesel worked. These passenger locomotives were consequently redundant and were sold to the Dutch State Railways. Freight working continues with the corresponding 26000 mixed traffic class. This view was taken in December 1950 near Oughtibridge showing No 27003, later named *Diana*, with the Liverpool-Harwich boat train.

Britain's first main line diesel electric locomotive was built by the English Electric Locomotive Co to the design of Mr H. A. Ivatt in 1947. It appeared just before nationalisation in sufficient time to carry the initials LMS. A second one followed in 1948. Both
were withdrawn in the later 1960s. This view shows the two of them hauling a Scottish
express through the beautiful Westmorland fells some time in 1949.

The Bo-Bo electric locomotives introduced in 1959, of which 200 were built to several
slight variations in design, now work all the express passenger trains and most of the
freight between London, Crewe, Liverpool and Manchester. More will be required
when the electrification to Glasgow is completed. No E3051 working a down freight
train through Berkhamsted in 1966. Rather extraordinarily, none of these engines, which
must be regarded as the crack main line express locomotives of today, has so far been
graced with the dignity of a name. (*Opposite*)

An experimental Fell diesel mechanical engine which was not a success. Built at Derby in 1951, it was a 2–D–2 (or could be described as 4–8–4 under the old Whyte notation), but the centre coupling rods were soon removed, thus making it a 4–4–4–4, or 2–B–B–2. It was withdrawn in 1958 after disgracing itself by catching fire in Manchester Central station. Seen here in January 1952 near Duffield on a train between Derby and Manchester.

The Southern was also early in experimenting with main line diesel electric locomotives, two engines, Nos 10201 and 10202, being built at Ashford in 1951, followed by a third No 10203 with increased horsepower, in 1954. The last mentioned is seen here passing Andover Junction on a down express on 14 May 1955, while the ancient Beattie tank No 30587, brought up specially from Cornwall to work a rail tour on the Bulford branch, runs into the station from the sidings. The SR did not proceed further with these experiments and, it being found uneconomic to maintain only three such engines in this way, they were later transferred to the LM region.

The experimental *Deltic*, built by English Electric, seen here at No 1 platform at Euston in 1956 on one of its first appearances. It was tried out exhaustively for several years on both the west and east coast main lines and underwent several modifications, eventually forming the basis of the D9000 class now used on the principal trains between Kings Cross and Edinburgh. This original prototype was never taken into BR stock and is now to be seen in the Science Museum, Kensington.

Another earlier design of diesel which did not come up to expectations. Twenty of these Co-Bo type (note the four and six wheeled bogies) were built by Metropolitan Vickers in 1958. They were allocated to the London Midland region and were at first tried out hopefully, working in pairs, on the newly introduced *Condor* express freight service, which started operations on 16 March 1959 between London and Glasgow. This consisted of a train of roller-bearing flat wagons conveying containers, which could be collected in the afternoon and delivered the following morning for an inclusive cost of £16 for a small container or £18 for a large one. This was a forerunner of the *Freightliner*, later to be introduced by Dr Beeching. Unfortunately these engines were found to be too unreliable for this important service, and after a few other miscellaneous duties in the south (they even made a few appearances at Moorgate on the St Albans commuter trains) they were banished to the north west and spent the remainder of their existence on the comparatively less important workings on the Furness and Maryport & Carlisle sections.

The Peak class, introduced in 1959, was not a success, at least so far as the first ten engines Nos D1-D10 were concerned. They were intended for working the west coast main line, but their sojourn at Camden was short, and they were soon transferred to Toton and confined to freight work, where they still remain at the time of writing. Their modified successors, Nos D11-D193, have however proved to be one of the most successful of all the diesel electric classes, and they now work practically all the principal services of the former Midland main lines between St Pancras and Carlisle, and between Leeds and Bristol. No D2 *Helvellyn*, one of the originals, seen here leaving St Pancras on 6 July 1960 with the 4.25 pm train to Manchester.

One of the earlier types of diesel electric shunters with jackshaft drive introduced by the LMS in 1939. Seen here shunting at Willesden in 1948, repainted British Railways, but still with its LMS number prefixed 'M', a temporary arrangement before the renumbering scheme was formulated, under which it became No 12030.

Early in the field of diesel railcars were three sets of four wheelers built by the British United Traction Co. They were tried out on various local services on the LM region, such as the Stanmore and the Watford to St Albans branches. A driving motor coach is seen here at Watford on 16 May 1956. They were exceedingly rough riding and uncomfortable, and disappeared around 1960.

Three car diesel on a Middlesbrough–Scarborough train on 23 July 1958. It is climbing from Whitby Town to Whitby West Cliff to rejoin the through line to Scarborough (seen on the viaduct, now closed and abandoned).

Even diesels require water! Not only for engine cooling purposes but also for supplying steam for train heating. Before the virtual disappearance of water troughs after the abandonment of steam haulage, some of the earlier diesels were even fitted with water pick up apparatus.

Experiments were also carried out with gas turbine propulsion, notably by the Western region, a Swiss built Brown Boveri design of type A1AA1A No 18000 being turned out in 1949, and a Co-Co, No 18100, being built by Metropolitan-Vickers in 1951 to Hawksworth's design. Outwardly these were of conventional diesel outline, but of a very different character, and much more resembling a steam locomotive in appearance, was this 4–6–0 built in 1961 by English Electric. Embodying gas turbine and mechanical gearbox transmission with flexible drive to the coupled wheels, its number was GT3. It does not appear to have been very successful, and after undergoing various trials, mostly on the old GCR main line, it faded out of existence. Seen here passing Ashby Magna on 21 September 1961.

Rolling Stock

One of Mr Bulleid's highly original ideas, a buffet car with an interior modelled as far as possible on the lines of the good old English pub with its highly individual atmosphere, and with exterior complete with imitation brickwork and tavern sign. *At the Sign of the Three Plovers*, vehicle No S7897. Photographed at Clapham Junction in July 1951.

One of the two Pullman observation cars converted for working the *Devon Belle* between Waterloo and Ilfracombe, seen here on the up train passing Exmouth Junction in July 1949. For some reason this particular service never caught on. One of these cars is now in the USA on tour with the *Flying Scotsman*, and the other, after being transferred to the Scottish region for use on the Kyle of Lochalsh line, has now found a home on the Dart Valley Railway. It has been entirely refurbished, complete with bar, which under the curious licensing laws of this country can serve drinks at any time of the day while the car is in traffic.

Dr Beeching's nightmare! This acutely business minded man, in his temporary capacity of responsibility for BR's finance, could not bear from his strictly actuarial point of view to see equipment lying idle for the major part of its existence and earning no revenue. A true banker's outlook, but unfortunately not quite geared to appreciate the fact that a transport industry must be able to cope with wide variations of traffic density and requirements. An extreme example of this is here well depicted by a scene in 1954, on the MR Bedford-Northampton branch, between Olney and Turvey, where at this time one of the two tracks of the double line was given over to the storage of about 200 coaches. Many of these were older vehicles of pregrouping days, which were brought out once a year during the height of the holiday season to be used perhaps only on seven or eight occasions at the weekend peaks. This particular location was eventually found to be impracticable, owing to its lonely situation, for it was discovered by the 'get-rich-quick' boys to be an easy source of obtaining valuable items such as batteries. This was apart from actual damage by purely senseless acts of vandalism which have so bedevilled the country in recent years. The notice board illustrates the almost indestructible permanence of such reminders of pregrouping days, still to be seen here and there where they have not already been removed or acquired for 'preservation' often by unknown sources.

The old time five-a-side compartment is now almost extinct, except on certain GNR suburban services out of Kings Cross and some multiple unit trains. It was difficult to photograph such a compartment in the very restricted space, but this view, taken in 1957, serves as a reminder of the old type of drop window operated by a leather strap. A substitute for this had in any case to be found in recent years owing to the fact that the straps made useful material for boot repairs and other purposes! The coach was a former LSWR bogie first/third composite (scrapped December 1957). Note the provision of special smoking accommodation, a former practice now completely reversed.

Six wheeled coaches in ordinary passenger service were already a rarity at nationalisation. Usually only to be found on country branches, they even disappeared from these in the early 1950s. Their last use is believed to have been on the old Mid Suffolk Light Railway, closed on 28 July 1952. Former Great Eastern vehicles, First/ Third Compo No E63404 (built at Stratford 1897 as GER 535) and brake Third No E62331 (Stratford 1901, GER 944) seen at Laxfield on 1 September 1951.

Privately chartered vehicles, such as this one, exclusively reserved for the conveyance of the humble sausage, have practically disappeared, except in a few specialised industries such as the large motor and oil companies, and for cement, etc. The once ubiquitous private owners' wagons were taken over as a whole by BR at nationalisation.

The conveyance of animals by rail is now virtually no more, and the once familiar horsebox is almost a forgotten sight. Gone are the days when race meetings at Newmarket would involve the running of special trains of horseboxes of the type shown in this illustration, taken at Aberayron in 1958.

Even more rare, and in fact now practically non-existent, is the sight of cattle or sheep voicing their protests at their uncomfortable and draughty journeys in the cattle wagons of yesteryear. This view at Holyhead shows a typical transhipment scene between Great Britain and Ireland.

The old time wooden goods wagon has little place in this day's railway world, and is virtually extinct, at any rate on the main lines. This picture is included as it depicts a glimpse of what happens to all good engines on their way to the locomotive 'Valhalla', wherever that may be. Taken at Gorton in 1948, it shows the last mortal remains of one of Robinson's fine pair of 4–6–0s of 1903, No 1479, originally GCR No 195 and later LNER 5195.

Civil Engineering

Several railway viaducts have been taken out of use during the last decade, and most of them demolished, among which may be mentioned two particularly fine ones in South Wales, Crumlin and Walnut Tree (both illustrated in the author's 'Wales and the Welsh Border Counties' by the present publishers). Other examples are Belah on the NER Barnard Castle–Kirkby Stephen line, and more recently the impressive viaduct shown here over the River Okement at Meldon, on the old LSWR, now out of use, but still in situ at the time of writing.

Viaduct at Dowery Dell, Hunnington, on the old Halesowen Railway, jointly operated by the LMS and GWR and closed in 1964. Since 1919 only freight trains and workmen's passenger services for employees at the Austin motor works at Longbridge, had been operated. The viaduct was subject to severe weight restrictions necessitating the use of light engines such as the Midland Kirtley goods No 22579 of 1868, a few of which were retained specifically for this duty until the later 1940s, after which it was found possible to use the slightly heavier Johnson engines, of not quite such ancient origin, but still very elderly. The viaduct is now demolished.

Robert Stephenson's fine Britannia tubular bridge over the Menai Straits, completed in 1850, narrowly escaped irreparable destruction from fire on 23 May 1970, this view being taken shortly afterwards. It formed part of the principal rail link between Great Britain and Ireland, and it was necessary to divert the shipping route from Holyhead to Heysham. It is however being rebuilt with a single line only and should again be in operation by the time this book is published.

The swing bridge over the River Nene at Sutton Bridge, on the Midland & Great Northern Joint Railway, served both road and a single line of railway. When this was closed in 1959 the rail section was converted for use as a second lane of roadway.

Another rail to road conversion, the bridge at Connell Ferry on the Ballachulish branch of the former Caledonian Railway, closed in March 1966. In this case road traffic had to be halted during the passage of a train.

When the former MS & LR was electrified between Manchester and Sheffield and Wath at the beginning of the 1950s, the old notorious twin tunnels at Woodhead constructed by Joseph Locke with great difficulty over a century before, were permanently closed and replaced by a new double-line tunnel alongside. One of the originals was reopened in 1965 to accommodate power cables, again not an easy project owing to accumulated deposits of soot of more than a hundred years, but the job was finished in 1969. This view was taken in 1946, and shows the old portals at the western end, with a 'Green Arrow' 2–6–2 on a train bound for Manchester.

Experiments with pre-fabricated track laying methods, first tried out by the LMS in 1938 on one of its Peterborough lines (whether MR or LNWR is not certain), were suspended during the war and resumed in 1945. This view shows a typical early scene at Berkhamsted, be it noted with steam crane, in May 1948. Such equipment would be impracticable now where there are overhead electric cables and girders, and modified designs have had to be employed which can work under the wires.

Stations

Moorgate, showing the terminal platforms used by the residential services for the MR and GNR lines. These services, which gave direct access to the city area, were suspended during the war.

This view, taken in 1945 before the platforms were renovated for resumption of services, shows City & South London electric locomotive No 36, which had been preserved on a plinth. Unfortunately it was found to be in such poor condition owing to exposure that it had to be broken up. A similar engine is however preserved in South Kensington Museum. The two derelict platforms were again brought into use on 6 May 1946 on the resumption of the GNR suburban service.

Stratford during reconstruction, 1946, in preparation for the extension of the Underground Central line to Hainault over what was formerly the GER Fairlop loop line. The LT lines at this point run underground, as shown by the incline (left) down to the tunnel. The main lines run through the middle distance beyond the signal cabin, to the left of which can be seen the former Loughton line and Lea Bridge platforms.

Several fine stations have been closed in recent years. An example is Snow Hill, Birmingham, on the Great Western's route to Shrewsbury and Chester, seen here with an express from Paddington to Birkenhead on 12 August 1961. Among others may be mentioned St Enoch, Glasgow. Both of these stations were conveniently sited in the heart of their respective cities. Another such was Nottingham Victoria, illustrated on page 124.

The new Euston emerging from the ashes of the old, with which it has not the slightest resemblance. The top illustration taken on 4 July 1964 shows an up express on the eastern (arrival) side, the train engine being diesel No D293, which had failed at Willesden and had had to be brought in by 2–6–0 No 78019.

The lower picture, 17 April 1964, shows the 5.27pm semi-fast to Rugby, in charge of No D5001, standing at platform No 10, one of the oldest parts of the station, and then shortly to be demolished to make way for the new edifice, already partly completed on the left on the site of the old platforms 6 and 7. Platform 9, on the site occupied by the Nissen Hut, was the old 'York' platform, once used by Midland trains.

Old Euston. Platform 5 and the short No 4, used mainly by electric trains to Watford and the outer suburban steam service. The train shown is the 7.31am from Tring with engine 80068 after having disgorged its commuting passengers. It was one of the trains involved in the Harrow accident mentioned elsewhere. This view was taken five years later in 1957.

The new Euston, as seen from the air. The only comparable feature with the old station is the general arrangement of the platforms, Nos 1-8 (reading from the left) being used by main line trains, usually arrivals, Nos 9 and 10 (note third rail electrified lines) by the local Watford service, 10 and 11 by the outer suburban and semi-main line EMU's, and the remaining west side platforms for main line departures.

Old Euston. The magnificent Great Hall with its beautiful decorated ceiling, all presided over by the fine statue of George Stephenson. This has been preserved elsewhere, but all else had to be destroyed when the station was rebuilt, a tragic and irreplaceable loss.

New Euston. Platforms 5 and 6, on the arrival of an 'inter-city' express.

The small wayside station on a main line is a fast disappearing feature of the railway scene, as local services which served these stations have been largely withdrawn. This view, taken on 23 April 1958, is typical of such. It shows a stopping train to Hereford at Tram Inn with GWR No 7011 *Banbury Castle*. Another train in the opposite direction has just departed. The local passenger service ceased on 9 June 1958 and the goods yard was closed on 5 October 1964. Tram Inn was on the main line between Shrewsbury and Worcester and South Wales. The station took its name from an adjacent inn, which no doubt came into existence in connection with the construction of the old tramroad. In the earlier part of the nineteenth century this consisted of three separate undertakings which formed a continuous link of twenty-five miles between Abergavenny and Hereford, largely parallel to the route of the present railway. It was of course laid with plate-rails and worked by horses.

One of those oddities, of which there have been a number of examples in the past, of a station without outside access, other than by means of a footpath. Such stations were purely for interchange purposes between one train and another. Cairnie Junction, on the old Great North of Scotland Railway, was served by trains between Aberdeen and Elgin, by both the coast road via Tillynaught (junction for Banff) and the inland route via Keith, where contact was made with the Highland Railway and Craighellachie (junction for the Speyside line). This had been advertised as an 'exchange platform only' until 13 June 1965, when it assumed the status of a normal station, only to be closed entirely on 6 May 1968. The illustration shows No 80121 awaiting a connecting train on 10 July 1957.

Bala Junction on the GWR mid-Wales line (now closed) was also unadvertised as a station in the public timetables. Roudham Junction on the GER, junction of the one time Thetford & Watton Rly, was also an interchange station only, without booking facilities. Other stations without road access, but which did have booking facilities, were Dovey Junction, on the Cambrian, and Riccarton Junction, on the NBR Waverley route, interchange point for the Hexham branch.

Fittleworth, typical country branch station on the old LB & SCR between Pulborough and Midhurst. Passenger service was withdrawn 7 February 1955, and the line completely closed on 6 May 1963. Sir Edward Elgar, one of the country's greatest musicians, spent his last days at Fittleworth.

Unusual station decorations on the platform at Verney Junction on the LNWR Bletchley–Oxford line. It no longer has a passenger service.

Distinctive type of station name-board designed to attract the attention of road users. Even at this time (1958) when there were about ten trains in each direction daily, the chances of a stranded motorist or weary hiker coming across this possible means of succour at the right place and time would be extremely unlikely. Nowadays, with the service reduced to but two trains to Birmingham in the early morning and two returning in the evening, the chances must be remote in the extreme.

Branch Lines

The purely dead end branch line, formerly such a distinctive feature of the railway network, has now almost completely disappeared, and even the secondary cross-country routes with connections at either end are somewhat few and far between, particularly in some parts of the country. Even where these still exist, they are of course worked by the inevitable diesel railcars, and such a pleasant experience as depicted in this illustration is now unfortunately only a memory except on privately preserved lines. It is taken on the Thaxted branch train, leaving Elsenham on 30 June 1951 behind Great Eastern 0–6–0T No 68530.

The midday Oxford–Fairford train taking water at Witney on 2 February 1957.

This L & YR steam rail motor was the last of a type of vehicle tried out by many railways before World War I for branch line work, particularly by this railway and the GWR. It was the only one to last just into nationalisation days. Seen here at Horwich in April 1947 on the branch train from Blackrod.

94

Seaton, Devon, Southern Railway, 9 July 1949, with the through Saturdays only coaches to Waterloo, to be attached to a main line train at Seaton Junction, headed by Adams 4-4-2T No 3488 (now to be seen on the Bluebell Railway). These engines were normally employed on the Lyme Regis branch, one for a week at a time, and it was found convenient to arrange the changeover from Exmouth Junction shed on a Saturday, when the taking-over engine could work an extra turn on the Seaton branch during its journey to Axminster. The regular branch service was worked by a pull-and-push set.

Another Seaton, this time in Rutland, junction for the Uppingham branch. This shows the small one-engine shed, the branch diverging to the left with the main line (now also closed) from Market Harboro' to Peterborough in the foreground. The engine is Ivatt 2-6-2T No 41214. By a curious coincidence, not only were these two widely separated Seatons, which both lost their passenger services in 1966, among the last steam worked branches in the country, but, more than that, saw the last pull-and-push motor trains.

Although not a branch line, this view shows a scene typical of the GWR in particular, which constructed a large number of unstaffed halts on branches and in some cases on main lines, where they could be situated close to local centres of population to encourage this type of traffic. 0–4–2T No 1464 on a Chalford–Gloucester motor train leaves Cashes Green Halt on 24 April 1958, quite evidently at the end of school time.

The Talyllyn Railway in its last years of operation before being rescued by the Preservation Society, the first of its kind. Taken at Abergynolwyn in 1948. The character in the wagon (fitted with improved seating), is the author, now unfortunately very many years older, the picture being taken by his son, at that time not quite twelve years of age.

One of the last of the Colonel Stephens lines to remain open was the Shropshire & Montgomery, and this owed its survival to the fact that it was used by the War Department during World War II. This view was taken from the rear brake van of a rail tour on 21 September 1958 passing through Shoot Hill station (not used by passengers since 1933), witnessed by a small but very charming audience.

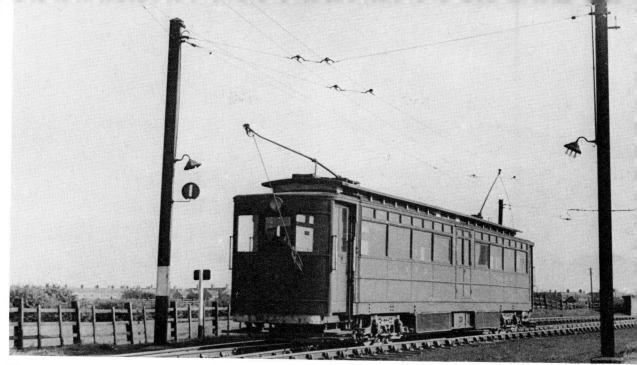

The Grimsby & Immingham, although operated by electric tramcars, was not an urban street tramway but ran over open countryside on conventional railway track, except at the Grimsby terminal which was in the street and the rail had to be sunk into the roadway in normal tram fashion. It was owned successively by the Great Central, LNER, and BR. This view shows a car at Cleveland Bridge in 1946.

Not exactly a branch line, but one of the few independent systems after nationalisation, the Liverpool Overhead was the only elevated city railway in the country. In spite of its obvious advantages in relieving road congestion, it was closed and dismantled after the end of 1956. Scene at Pier Head on 19 April 1950.

Ireland

British Railways at nationalisation on 1 January 1948 still retained an interest in certain of the lines either wholly or partly in Northern Ireland, notably the Northern Counties Committee. Until that time it was under the ownership of the LMS which had inherited it at the grouping from the Midland. This company in turn had many years before acquired the old Belfast & Northern Counties Railway. Under Midland and LMS ownership the line had gradually acquired many of these companies' characteristics, noticeably the adoption of the well known crimson lake livery for all of the engines, both passenger and goods, along with other sundry typical Derby features.

This view shows one of a class of fifteen 2–6–0s built for express passenger work between 1933 and 1942. This particular one, No 93 *The Foyle*, was actually constructed at Derby in 1933 and is seen here passing Coleraine on a Londonderry express. The right-hand running is due to an excellent practice on this line of arranging the passing loops bi-directionally in order that non-stop trains either way can take the straight road to avoid speed reduction. Note also the somersault signals used by this railway, as on some lines in this country, noticeably the Great Northern and the M & GNJR. The 4–4–0 No 77 on the left, it will be noted, has many distinctive Midland features.

BR interests in the old NCC passed to the newly formed Ulster Transport Authority on the creation of that body in August 1948.

(*Below*) Another line under LMS ownership was the 3ft 0in gauge between Londonderry and Strabane, where it joined with the County Donegal Railways Joint Railways Joint Committee, and in practice was worked by them as part of its own system. It passed to the UTA, but this concern was not interested in maintaining railways of this nature, and it was closed at the end of 1954. This scene shows the terminus at Londonderry, with one of the large 2-6-4Ts of the CDRJC.

The Dundalk, Newry & Greenore was another late survivor of English ownership, having LNWR origins. The engines and stock were pure North Western, as can be seen in this view taken in 1950, where the railway crossed the GNR main line on the level. This engine is No 4 *Newry*, built at Crewe in 1876. BR eventually decided that they were not prepared to subsidise the line any longer, and it was closed at the end of 1951.

In the last years of its independent existence that enterprising railway, the Great Northern of Ireland, introduced five new express 4-4-0s in 1948 for working its crack expresses between Belfast and Dublin. They were the last of this once universal type to be built in the British Isles—possibly in the whole world. No 208 *Lagan* is seen passing Dundalk in 1950.

The last horse-worked passenger branch in the British Isles was to be found at Fintona in Northern Ireland, as late as 1957, when all the lines in the area were completely closed by the Ulster Transport Authority. This short three-quarter mile branch was operated so far as the passenger services were concerned throughout its 104 years of existence by horse traction. This view, taken in 1948, shows the tramcar type vehicle which had been in use for many years (it is now in the Belfast Museum). Although nominally of the usual three classes, 1st and 2nd, with 3rd on the upper deck, these were in practice meaningless, and were occupied according to the prevailing meteoric conditions. The Irish have but two standards of weather, viz a 'soft' day, when it is raining, or a 'grand' day, when it is not. The only passenger on this trip in 1948 who had bothered to ascend to the upper regions was the author's son, then aged eleven. The charming little Irish 'colleens' obviously took much interest in the proceedings, and the motive power was going all out at fully 5mph.

Interchange at a busy country junction, a sight almost now forgotten in these days of little more than the extremes of 'inter-city' expresses and workers' commuter services. This 1955 scene, at the famous Limerick Junction in Ireland, can in fact still be experienced. It is reminiscent of somewhat similar junction interchange points in this country, mostly now no more, when great activity, resulting from trains from various destinations being timed to meet more or less simultaneously, was interspersed with periods of inactivity. One particularly calls to mind such places as Melton Constable, on the now defunct M & GNJR.

Running Sheds

A side effect of electrification and dieselisation is the almost complete disappearance of the old time running shed, with its turntable, coaling and watering facilities, and provision for ash removal, etc, none of which are required by the new forms of motive power. This to say nothing of the personnel—shedmaster, assistant foremen, clerical staff, fitters, coalers, cleaners, lighters up, and so on. All but the smallest sheds had varying degrees of repair facilities. Electric and diesel locomotives can simply be locked up and left in any convenient location, and for maintenance need only a few specialised depots at fairly widely separated centres. A few former steam sheds here and there are still used for housing diesel locomotives, but most have been razed to the ground and the sites used for other purposes. This view shows Watford, 9 March 1949, typical of a smaller shed with an allocation of about twenty engines, in this case mainly tanks for working the outer suburban services between Euston, Tring and Bletchley. There were usually about thirteen of these, such as No 42668, seen here with a smaller 2–6–2T No 40010, which was one of four pull-and-push fitted engines used on the St Albans and Stanmore branches. This shed, in common with many others, has now been entirely demolished and the site converted to a car park for the use of commuters and other rail travellers.

(below) Larger sheds constructed on the roundhouse principle, with a central turntable giving access to any particular bay, were favoured by some railways, notably the Midland, Great Western and North Eastern. This view of Selby taken in 1948 shows large 4–8–0T shunter No 9914, 0–8–0 class Q5 No 63286, and others. This type of shed had of course the disadvantage that if the table became damaged or was out of action for any unforeseen reason all the engines were trapped and immobilised.

101

Roundhouses were usually totally enclosed (some of the largest had two or three circles, interconnected), but there were also a few of the open type, more often encountered abroad. Probably the best known of these was the one at Inverness, where many historic photographs of Highland engines have been taken in the past. This, taken on 15 June 1960, was undoubtedly one of the last of such, when the restored Jones 4–6–0 No 103 was taking part in a week's railtour of Scotland. Note the powered turntable, worked from the vacuum pipe on the engine.

Other open roundhouses were to be found at such scattered points as Carlisle (Upperby), Middlesbrough, Horsham, and St Blazey in Cornwall. Guildford was a curious combination of half a circle of separate bays, together with a four road straight shed, only accessible via the turntable.

Primitive coaling operation still in use at Fratton in 1957 (a roundhouse jointly shared in pre-grouping days by the LSWR and LB & SCR). The engine is standard class 4 2–6–0 No 76019.

The most usual type of coaling plant before the introduction of the modern principle was this elevated staging, served by an incline for the passage of wagons. The coal had to be transferred to the small tubs, a tedious man-handling operation, and tipped into the tender or bunker of the engine below. Scene at Ashford in 1952. This illustration clearly shows the 'hungry lion and wheel' emblem used by BR in its earlier years.

For a number of years prior to the war, most large sheds had been provided with the modern type of coaling plant such as this at York. The loaded coal wagon was hauled bodily to the top, where it would be up-ended to discharge its load into a hopper. Suitable chutes directed the coal to the engine's tender or bunker below, a simple and speedy process.

Accidents

Tragedy at Bourne End crossing, between Berkhamsted and Boxmoor, 30 September 1945. The up night express from Perth, for reasons never fully elucidated, took the crossover at high speed instead of reducing to twenty mph, and plunged down the embankment. Several hours later efforts were still being made to extricate the trapped passengers.

Four weeks later, the engine, unrebuilt Royal Scot No 6157 *The Royal Artilleryman*, was successfully raised and rerailed, the embankment having to be shored up before this could be done. The engine was then taken first to Willesden and later to Crewe for rebuilding. This was an unlucky engine in this area, for five years later, on 16 November 1950, No 46157, now in its rebuilt form, bent a connecting rod while working the 8.30 pm postal through Berkhamsted. This rendered the engine completely immoveable, and caused several hours delay. The train itself was eventually drawn back to Boxmoor, where it could be transferred to the slow line, and proceeded northwards over two hours late. A fitters van arrived at 1.00 am to work on 46157, which was towed away about 2.00 am.

The disastrous accident at Harrow on 8 October 1952, in which 112 passengers and enginemen lost their lives. This was the second most serious accident in the history of the railways of Great Britain, exceeded only by the notorious Gretna disaster of 1915, when the loss of life totalled 227. At Harrow the up sleeping car train from Perth ran at full speed into the rear of the 7.31 am Tring to Euston train, which was just leaving the station after making its last call. Before anything could be done this wreckage was ploughed into by the 8.00 am express from Euston, with the results shown in this picture. Somewhere underneath all that pile would be what remained of the rear two coaches of the local, in which the author regularly travelled, and which only by a merciful providence was he not on board on this particular day. The engine visible is No 46202 *Princess Anne*, only recently rebuilt from turbine to ordinary reciprocal propulsion, in which form it had an exceedingly brief life as it was damaged beyond repair. So too was its pilot, Jubilee No 45637 *Windward Islands*. The real villain of the piece, No 46242 *City of Glasgow*, got off more lightly and was repaired and returned to traffic.

Miscellany

The post-war restored 'Flying Scotsman' proudly displays its headboard, and is seen here running into Edinburgh Waverley on 24 April 1948. On the right is NBR D32 4-4-0 No 2451. The train engine is Gresley Pacific No 4 *William Whitelaw*.

Under the LNER's 1946 renumbering scheme the A4 streamlined Pacifics took the numbers 1 to 34, although not, as with other classes, in order of construction. Those bearing directors' names had to come first, starting with No 1 *Sir Ronald Matthews*.

Early in 1948 a number of trials were organised over the principal main lines with engines of other companies' designs to decide on future policy for new locomotive construction. This view shows LNER Gresley A4 Pacific No 60034 *Lord Faringdon* working the down Midland Region 'Royal Scot' on 19 May 1948, about to enter Northchurch Tunnel.

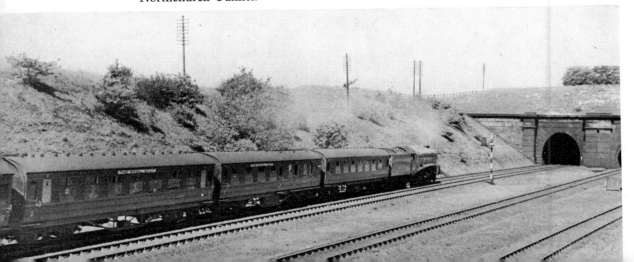

Although engines usually kept to their native systems, it sometimes happened that a shortage of motive power could result in temporary loan from one region to another. Here is SR Pacific No 34039 *Boscastle*, lent to the Eastern Region, working an up express from Norwich, seen at Ipswich on 1 September 1951.

The short lived oil burning experiment of 1947, SR T9 4–4–0 No 121, seen here being refuelled at Eastleigh through the medium of Stroudley 0–4–2T No 2244, adapted as a pumping unit.

Commuters' train, Southern Railway, during the war years. At Waterloo in 1941 a suburban train has just arrived. Unhurriedly the homeward bound workers find their seats. Raid or no raid, it will leave to time. Only a bomb—they would call it an incident—will stop it or them getting through. Incidentally the train is composed of the earlier formation of SR electric trains, with two intermediate trailers between a couple of three car motor sets. These were later modified, and the units reformed into four coach sets.

Commuters' train, LMS, just after the war. Outer surburban train from Euston to Bletchley at Watford on 12 September 1946, with LNWR Prince of Wales 4-6-0 No 25752, one of several which were reprieved from scrap during the war years for such secondary duties. Although the local passenger trains on this line were few and far between during off peak periods, it had a very good and adequate morning and evening business service, conveniently timed and with no overcrowding. The good riding locomotive-hauled coaching stock was some of the most comfortable on any of the London lines.

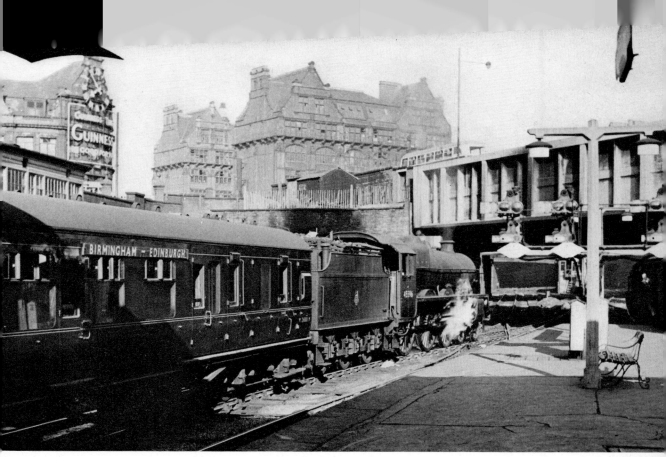

Birmingham New Street, on 29 June 1957, before reconstruction, with the through train to Edinburgh about to depart behind Jubilee No 45596 *Bahamas* (now preserved at Dinting Railway Centre). The once almost universal use of the useful destination boards on the coaches has now been almost entirely abandoned, and it is difficult to distinguish one train from another. A very retrograde step, and a sad reflection that this impersonal age has reduced even our finest trains almost to anonymity. Such old-established famous names as the Irish Mail, the Flying Scotsman, the Cornish Riviera, together with many others of rather more recent origin, such as the Golden Arrow, Royal Highlander, East Anglian, Thames-Clyde Express, and many others, are all becoming little more than a memory of more gracious days. They no longer appear proudly displayed on the trains themselves, even though a few do still receive an almost grudging minimal mention in the public timetables. They are more often referred to as just the 10.00 from Kings Cross, or whatever.

The slip coach, a facility which has now entirely disappeared. It was revived to some extent by the GWR after the war in 1946. This view shows the main part of the *Cornish Riviera*, after ridding itself of its tail, approaching Heywood Junction, Westbury, on 24 August 1956. The slip coach, under control of the guard, would come to a stand short of the junction of the avoiding line, which the main train would have taken, and subsequently be drawn into the station by a shunting engine. In other instances where no divergence of route would be involved, the slip coach would normally be allowed to run into the station platform under the guard's operation. The Great Western was the principal user of slip coaches, the last of which was at Bicester North, off the down train from Paddington to Wolverhampton, finally discontinued on 9 September 1960.

The famous 8.30 pm postal from Euston, picking up mail bags at Berkhamsted on 28 June 1947. Photographs such as this were difficult to obtain, as these trains invariably operated during the night. This one was only possible, even on one of the longest day-light days of the year, by the incidence of 'double summer time', by which the clock was advanced by two hours as a war time expedient.

This method of collecting and dispatching mail bags, first introduced in the latter part of the nineteenth century, latterly fell into disuse and was completely abandoned towards the end of 1971.

The old time loose coupled pick-up goods train is now becoming a rare sight, with the closure of so many local yards and sidings and more concentration on central railheads with increasing distribution by road. This picturesque view shows class 4 goods No 44026 (incidentally the last new engine to be built for the old Midland Railway) on Monsal Dale viaduct, on the beautiful main line through the Peak District which is unfortunately now entirely closed.

Another charming scene, this time on the Severn Valley line, near Bridgnorth, on 30 August 1962. The engine is GWR 2–6–2T No 4129. With the increasing use of continuous braked wagons for freight trains the old time brake van is now a disappearing feature and can be dispensed with on a fully braked train. The goods guard, sometimes irreverently but one hopes affectionately referred to among railwaymen as 'Tail-end-Charlie' now travels with the enginemen on the locomotive.

This route was also closed by BR, although part of it has been reopened under private enterprise in the form of the Severn Valley Railway Company Limited.

Level crossing—old style. This is actually a war time picture taken on 25 June 1941, and shows MR class 3 0–6–0 No 3368 at Breadsall Crossing, near Derby. The white-washed tyres and wings on the author's car are a reminder of a common practice at this time to provide extra visibility for other road users in the blackout.

A level crossing where a busy road has to cross a main line. There are in fact two crossings only a couple of hundred yards apart, the second being just obscured by the coaches of the pull-and-push train leaving Poole for Bournemouth in 1960. This always seemed to be a particularly dangerous point, as down trains from Branksome would be charging down the one in sixty gradient and dependent entirely on the two signalmen being able to get their gates closed against the continual stream of road traffic in time. Fortunately no accident has ever occurred.

Level crossing, new style, in picturesque setting at Brockenhurst. This is operated from the signal box in the usual way, but the increasing use of unmanned crossings of the half barrier type has come under a good deal of criticism since the disastrous Hixon accident of 6 January 1968, referred to elsewhere.

Typical view of old time picturesque signal box, now a disappearing feature of the railway scene. Changing the staff at Kielder Forest, on the now closed Riccarton Junction to Hexham by-way of the old NBR in Northumberland, April 1952.

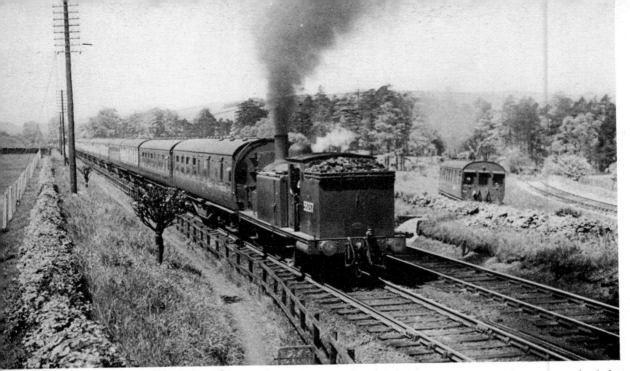

Beattock Bank, on the main Caledonian line between Carlisle and Glasgow, required the use of banking engines for all but the lightest trains. CR 0–4–4T No 55237 is seen here thus engaged, while on the right is the Moffat branch motor train.

Another incline picture. The boat trains on the Folkstone Harbour branch, with its gradient of one in thirty, were worked until 1959 (when they were replaced by GWR 0–6–0PTs) by elderly South Eastern Stirling 0–6–0Ts. A heavy train would require four engines, three at the front, as in this picture taken in August 1954, the fourth banking engine being out of sight.

While snow blockages occur in varying degree in this country during most winters particularly in the north, a typical event being illustrated on page 55, disruption by flooding is comparatively rare. In this scene, a Midland compound seems to be coping adequately at Nottingham on 19 March 1947, following heavy snowfalls in the month. The overbridge carried the former GCR main line, now closed.

A railway owned steamer, the *Princess Victoria*, which was built for the LMS by William Denny Bros Ltd in 1947, foundered off the County Down coast with the loss of 128 lives in the gale which swept over the British Isles on the morning of 31 January 1953. The boat was on the 7.45 sailing from Stranraer to Larne. A contributing if not major factor seems to have been the design of the bulkhead doors used for the embarkation of vehicles, which were rather curiously, and as it turned out disastrously, planned to open inwards. They burst open under the unusually high pressure of the water.

The modern method of handling bulk traffic. Loading a freightliner's containers on to specially designed bogie wagons for high speed transit between selected centres. One of Dr Beeching's progressive ideas.

Another popular innovation of recent years is the motor-rail car carrier to enable holiday motorists to travel to Scotland or other centres in comfort accompanied by their cars, and avoid the fatigue of a long and uninteresting drive. This view shows such a train making a brief halt, probably for engine or crew purposes, at Carlisle.

This type of double deck car carrier is also used to a considerable extent in conveying trains of anything up to a hundred cars from factory to other parts of the country, with the incidental benefits of great saving in time and man power and alleviation of road congestion.

State Occasions

Investiture of Prince Charles at Caernarvon on 1 July 1969. The Royal Train ran on this occasion from Euston to Griffiths Crossing, near Caernarvon.

Their Royal Highnesses Princess Anne and Prince Charles board the Royal Train at Euston on 30 June 1969. Seen, left to right, are Sir Henry Johnson, Chairman of BR, and behind him, partly obscured, is R. L. E. Lawrence, Esq., General Manager, Midland Region, the Prince and Princess being escorted by W. J. Griffin, Esq., Station Manager, Euston.

Arrival of the Royal Train near the site of the old Griffiths Crossing Halt, which had been closed in 1937. Her Majesty the Queen and the Duke of Edinburgh about to descend the steps.

Funeral train of King George the Sixth, 15 February 1952, about to leave Paddington for Windsor. The engine bears the name and number 4082 *Windsor Castle*, an engine which the King once drove on a visit to Swindon Works. Unfortunately the real *Windsor Castle* was in shops at the time, and the engine which actually worked the train was No 7013, with transferred name and number plates.

Sir Winston Churchill's last journey from Waterloo to Handborough (for Blenheim) seen here near Earley, on 30 January 1965, hauled by the engine bearing his immortal name.

Rail Tours

Not perhaps a particularly arresting photograph at first sight, but it does nevertheless have a certain special interest and significance. Taken on 15 April 1950, it was on the occasion of the first ever privately organised rail tour, sponsored by the Stephenson Locomotive Society, over any section of line not normally used by passenger trains. The view shows the train signalled at Spur Junction, on the SE & CR, between Beckenham Junction and Crystal Palace, over the single line loop, very rarely used, down to Norwood Junction, on the old LB & SCR. It was undoubtedly the first of many

thousands of similar carriage window views that were to be taken on the multitudinous rail tours which were to follow during the 1950s and 1960s.

Steam returns to the Inner Circle! Scene at Edgware Road on Sunday afternoon, 22 September 1957, when London Transport agreed to run a train to Hammersmith, back to Edgware Road, and thence making the round trip via South Kensington, Victoria, Aldgate, Baker Street, and finishing up at Wembley Park. Steam freight trains were still to be seen at various times along the northern half of the Circle line between Paddington and Farringdon Street, and no doubt Metropolitan engineering department works trains traversed the whole circuit during the small hours, but certainly no steam passenger train had been seen for very many years, and it was viewed with amazement by waiting passengers as it ran through the stations en route non stop. (There were of course the 'widened lines' between Kings Cross and Moorgate over which the residential trains for the Great Northern and Midland lines were steam worked until comparatively recently, and in addition the transfer goods traffic between the Eastern and Southern regions via Snow Hill).

A rail tour on 14 April 1957 over the old Leicester & Swannington Railway, opened in 1833, the oldest portion of what eventually became the Midland. Passenger trains had been discontinued since 1928. On this occasion it was not possible to travel through the tunnel into Leicester West Bridge owing to the restricted clearance being unable to take main line coaching stock, but this was achieved on a subsequent occasion with a train of brake vans.

A mammoth seven day tour in June 1960, organised by the Railway Correspondence and Travel Society and the Stephenson Locomotive Society, covered some 1250 miles in Scotland, including several branches which had not had a passenger service for a long time. Entirely steam worked, of course, and with a wide variety of engines, including the four which had been restored by the Scottish region to their pregrouping liveries for working enthusiasts' specials. These were the Highland Jones goods (illustrated on page 120), the Caledonian single, NBR No 256 *Glen Douglas*, and GNSR 49 *Gordon Highlander* seen here at the picturesque station of Monymusk, on the Alford branch, 13 June 1960. These engines are now in the Glasgow Transport Museum.

Rail tour enthusiasts were often not too particular with regard to standards of comfort, even if it meant riding in open goods wagons when it was not possible to provide passenger coaches. This view shows a special train on the Welshpool & Llanfair 2ft 6in gauge line in Wales, on 30 June 1956 before closure by the GWR, taking water at Melin Dolrhydd. Passenger services had been discontinued since 1931 (hence lack of coaches), but part of the line has now been reopened by the W & L Preservation Society.

Another trip necessitating the use of wagons, on the Cromford & High Peak mineral line, 1000 feet up in the wilds of Derbyshire. Its three inclines, two of them cable worked, precluded the possibility of any sort of passenger service. The line was closed in 1967 after a life of some 137 years. Photograph taken 25 April 1953.

An unforgettable very early rail tour, and one of the most ambitious efforts then conceived. It ran on 24 August 1952, and comprised a through train from Manchester to Hull and back. The main feature was the traversal of the old H & BR main line between Cudworth and Hull. There was at this time still a wide variety of most desirable vintage motive power available, and this trip employed NER class R (LNER D20) 4-4-0 No 62360, together with MR Johnson class 3 4-4-0 No 40726, the last to remain in traffic (it was withdrawn immediately after the tour). Seen here at Cudworth during the change over of engines on the return journey, the Midland taking over from the North Eastern for the run to Manchester.

The last through train over the LNWR line between Abergavenny Junction and Merthyr, skirting the northern edge of the South Wales coalfield, was a special organised by the Stephenson Locomotive Society on 5 January 1958. Webb coal tank No 58926 (now preserved in Penrhyn Castle Museum) and 0-8-0 No 49121 pause here for water at Brynmawr.

Rail tour in sylvan setting, even though on the outskirts of Birmingham, climbing through Handsworth Park on the Perry Bar–Soho line, on 25 May 1957.

Another memorable occasion, 2 December 1962, when two of the eighty-seven-year-old surviving Beattie 2–4–OTs were brought back from Cornwall to London. The class had not been seen here since they had been displaced on the suburban services seventy-five years earlier, apart from possible visits to Nine Elms works before these were moved to Eastleigh. The two little engines traversed the Hampton Court and Shepperton branches, in itself a golden opportunity to 'do' those long electrified lines by steam, and were relieved in between by a larger engine to run over the comparatively newly constructed line to Chessington, which had never had a steam service. This tour was so popular and over subscribed that it had to be repeated a fortnight later.

This was the end of the class, as all three were immediately withdrawn from service after their long reign on the Wenford Bridge line in Cornwall, for which they had been retained for more than sixty years after the last of their sisters, and during which time they had had several extensive rebuilds. They were supplanted there by some GWR 0–6–0PTs, which at last were found as a satisfactory long-sought substitute for the particular requirements of the line. The newcomers' reign was however short-lived as they were in turn very soon replaced by diesels. Fortunately two of the Beattie engines have been retained for preservation, one by British Railways, and the other by the Quainton Road Society.

By 1966 steam rail tours were becoming increasingly difficult to organise, and from London they were confined to departures from Waterloo, even if destined for the north. This they could do by means of the North and South Western Junction line and transfer to the GCR main line at Neasden.

One such, on 13 August 1966, is seen here, halting at Nottingham Victoria for change of engines. This is one of the large city stations referred to elsewhere, which is now entirely closed.

The last privately organised steam tours allowed by British Railways, of which there were several by different Societies, ran on 4 August 1968, but the final trip of all was run by British Railways themselves on 11 August 1968. This was from Manchester and Liverpool to Carlisle and back, via Blackburn and Ais Gill, over the Midland Railway Settle and Carlisle line. For the 314 mile trip the not inconsiderable fare of £15.75 was charged, but nevertheless the accommodation for 470 passengers was fully booked, an indication of the potential source of revenue which could accrue with similar trips today. Unfortunately, British Railways prefer to turn a blind eye to the past, normally such a particularly British sentiment and characteristic—witness, for instance, the annual veteran car race to Brighton. Steam rail-tours are becoming increasingly recognised in many other countries as an attractive advertising feature appertaining to railways in general and as this book goes to press there are at last some early signs that BR may after all come to realise this fact.

Pause for water at Hellifield, on the outward journey. The last 'Britannia' to remain in service *Oliver Cromwell*, No 70013, worked the major part of the journey, but was relieved in part by a couple of class 5s. At the finish of its duty *Oliver Cromwell* proceeded immediately to Norwich, where it was removed to join Alan Bloom's fine collection of preserved locomotives at Bressingham Hall, near Diss.

Arrival at Liverpool Lime Street on the evening of 11 August 1968 of the last commemorative steam trip. Stanier black 5 No 45110 performed the final honours, and is one of the twelve engines of the well known class acquired by various bodies for preservation.

Acknowledgements

As in previous works of this nature, I have first and foremost to tender my grateful thanks to Mr C. R. Clinker, well known as today's most qualified expert on British Railway history, who has again been kind enough to examine my script and to provide sundry additional information, together with many useful suggestions. Also to Mr J. Edgington, of BR Publicity, Euston, and again to my son, Mr R. M. Casserley, himself well versed in the subject and able to offer a number of useful comments. Again, not least to my wife, for her valiant efforts in deciphering my own peculiar brand of shorthand—which she prefers to describe as purely appalling writing—to say nothing of the many second and third thoughts which invariably follow the initial efforts (usually after they have been typed!). Most of the illustrations are from the author's own camera, but special acknowledgement must be made to the undermentioned in respect of photographs supplied.

BR Publicity, Paddington, 53, 54 (bottom), 57 (bottom), 58, 60, 63 (top); BR Publicity, Euston, 54, 55, 70 (top), 72 (top), 73 (bottom), 74 (top), 76, 81 (top), 83 (bottom), 89 (bottom), 90, 91, 105, 115 (bottom), 116, 117; Imperial War Museum, 51, 52, 56, 57 (top), 61 (bottom), 103 (top); J. Edgington, 124 (top); M. Mensing, 75 (bottom), 77, 87 (bottom), 109, 111 (bottom), 123; R. J. Buckley, 122 (bottom); J. Hardman, 71; P. J. Kelley, 118 (bottom); R. M. Casserley, 68 (bottom), 94 (centre).

Bibliography

Railway Magazine—various issues
Railway Handbook—various issues
Railway Observer—various issues
British Railway Steam Locomotives—E. S. Cox
The Last Steam Engineer, Riddles—Col H. C. B. Rogers
Bulleid, Last Giant of Steam—Sean Day Lewis
Transport Goes to War
British Railways in Wartime
Facts about British Railways in Wartime
British Railways in Peace and War
War on the Line—SR
The LMS at War
Timetable for Victory
History of British Railways during the War—Bell
British Railways Today and Tomorrow—Railway Executive 1949
Transport Act 1947—HM Stationery Office
London Plan Working Party's Report. 1949
Report on Electrification of Railways. 1951
Presentation of Relics and Records—Report to BTC 1951
Report of International Railway Congress. 1954
Reshaping of British Railways—British Railways Report 1963
The Great Isle of Wight Train Robbery
The Channel Tunnel 1802-1967—A. S. Travis

Index